CONTENTS

CHAPTER
Chicago Housing Authority
Police Taking Every Risk

FOREWORD

Crime and violence are nothing new to major metropolitan areas, but the culture of drug sales and gangs had become increasingly prevalent in suburban townships and rural areas. The plight of the poor and uneducated cannot be ignored. It becomes tragic for everyone when "inner city crimes" spill out of the areas where "those people live."

The aspirations of a man who wanted to provide a clean and safe environment for low-income families crossed paths with the dreams of another who was seeking to build a better life in an occupation he never imagined he would pursue. The crossroads that intersected their plans brought the author full circle. A child raised in public housing returns to serve and protect a new generation of its inhabitants. However, no matter how altruistic the motivation, some people cannot be

saved, and things are never as simple as they may seem.

PREFACE

The 1990s unfolded as a distinct chapter in American history, particularly for those of us in law enforcement. It was the era of the "war on drugs," a time when popular culture and youth trends shifted towards a fascination with street life, drug culture, and the gritty allure of criminality and thuggery. There have always been gangs and violence in human history. My friends against yours, my army against your army, my country, my culture, my religion against everything you trust and believe in. We struggle against each other at conception, trying to be the first to reach and fertilize the egg. Conflict and aggression are in our DNA.

In America, whether it was the English or French settlers versus the Native population, then the English upper class versus the Irish Mob, Chinese Tongs, Italian gangsters, there was friction. The emergence of White Power groups, 1%r Motorcycle clubs, or Black and Latino street gangs, there has always been "bad boys." Each new group of the underclass, desperate for their scrap of the American Dream, are willing to take it, if it could not be earned or obtained on their timetable.

The façade of the ultimate hero, the White Knight, started to fall after the 80's. Children stopped playing "Cowboys and Indians" or "Cops and Robbers," as the media and our morals blurred the lines between good versus evil. The Antihero became popular, while the image of being good for the sake of goodness became the rarity or the falsehood. Even the most famous comic book hero was killed off for being "too good." Everybody wanted to be the bad guy. Testosterone makes males aggressive; poverty, hopelessness and apathy has been proven to make us prey on our neighbors. There is also profit for everyone when you invest in crime.

Yet, beneath these visible currents, unseen forces were at play, pulling certain levers to target Black and Brown communities. Unknown to us at the time, American government officials assisted in flooding our inner-city streets with drugs, while arming law enforcement agencies across the country to the teeth with military style weapons and armor, unleashing them on the same communities they helped infect. Their plan pitted the poor and desperate against their paid protectors. Our trusted officials were purposely diverting the youth of these communities away from paths of positive growth, through popular music and messaging to feed the pipeline of privately owned prisons nationwide. It was difficult for many to avoid the allure of fast money, usually resulted in a swift and violent death, or the inevitable confines of incarceration.

Amidst this troubled landscape, law enforcement was also undergoing a transformation. Policing was no longer slave catching and buck breaking, but an arbiter for domestic and civil disputes. It remained a Whites only role infused with deep Irish roots for almost 100 years before any other race or sex were allowed to participate. Despite the historic milestone of the first Black man serving in the Chicago Police Department, dating back to 1872, the reality for Black officers was a stark contrast. They found themselves often relegated to desk duty, lock-up shifts, or any assignment that kept them away from patrols in predominantly White neighborhoods. It was a common tale for Black officers to respond to calls at White residences, only to be met with indifference or outright disdain from the occupants. The audacious demand of White citizens was a constant echo: "I want the Real Police!"—a statement that cut deep, and resonated within the ranks of Black officers.

The term "Real Police" reverberated through our days in the police academy, and whenever Chicago Police Officers graced our presence. To them, no other law enforcement entity in the country could lay claim to that title but them. However, the inaugural class of officers in the Chicago Housing Authority Police Department had a different story to tell.

With fewer than a hundred officers and supervisors, lacking proper vehicles, grappling with poor radio reception, and inundated with misinformation about their authority and jurisdiction, the first class of the CHAPD took to the streets with unwavering determination. Trained at the Timothy J. O'Connor Chicago Police Academy, under their required courses for state certification, the CHAPD was initially envisioned as a supplementary police force to support the Chicago Police Department, but they were wholly unwanted. Yet, the irony lay in the fact that all arrests made, and contraband seized by CHAPD were credited to the Chicago Police Districts. Local media coverage often attributed our work to the CPD, perpetuating the misconception that we were nothing more than contract security officers.

Despite the uphill battle, we stood firm in our commitment

to serve the residents with professionalism and integrity. The public perception remained—a persistent view of us as outsiders, overshadowed by the CPD, despite our hard work, federal funding, and empowerment.

Our superiors, many of them retired CPD officers, straddled a fine line between cooperation and a lingering loyalty to their former department. Their CHA stars remained pinned to their uniforms in lockers, while their CPD badges gleamed prominently as they departed for the day—a symbolic reminder of where their allegiances lay.

For the first class of CHAPD officers, unity was their strength. They stood shoulder to shoulder, facing every call and conflict with unwavering solidarity. When deployed into the unknown on foot patrol, they ventured into territories where CPD presence was minimal. Public Housing North, the notorious Cabrini Greens, and Public Housing South's Robert Taylor Homes were zones overlooked and purposely underserved by the CPD Calls for service often went unanswered, leaving residents in distress.

Enter the second class of CHAPD officers. We bolstered the numbers, allowing our more experienced colleagues to implement learned tactics and focus on problem areas with greater precision.

What follows are glimpses into the odd and humorous incidents I recall from my time on patrol—encounters with individuals who left an indelible mark in my mind as well as on my heart. In sharing these stories, I aim to convey the human side of policing, filled with imperfections and moments of growth. For every flaw and misstep, there was a lesson learned, shaping me into the officer I became.

Each day I donned that uniform, I did so with the sobering realization that I could meet my end in the line of duty, and I accepted it. A lot of newer cops are missing that. Policing, despite its troubling origins rooted in slave-catching and systemic oppression, remains a vital necessity. It calls upon the brave few to stand against forces that most shy away from, upholding a social contract that demands swift and judicious intervention in times of trouble.

Wielding such power demands an inherent responsibility—one that many falter in upholding fairly and impartially. These are the stories of my time in service, colored by the complexities of law enforcement, the human condition, and the unyielding pursuit of justice. Let us embark on this journey together.

ACKNOWLEDGEMENTS

I would like to acknowledge the following people and organizations whose unconditional support and encouragement were instrumental in making me the cop I was, and the person I am today: My mother, Audrey; the Chicago Public School System; the United States Marine Corps; the instructors at the Timothy J. O'Connor Chicago Police Academy; Vince Lane; Hosea Crossley; my Field Training Officer, the senior officers of the first class of the Chicago Housing Authority Police Department; my professors at the University of Wisconsin – Stout; and my loving wife, Bevin Faith Christie.

I would also like to express gratitude to the people I

served with, (Chicago Housing Authority Police Officers and Security), as I embarked on this life-altering journey into law enforcement. The odds were always against us, but we showed up every day to serve a community that needed and deserved better.

Chicago Housing Authority Police Taking Every Risk

C.H.A.P.T.E.R.

About the Author

 Rodney Craig Dukes was born in Chicago's Cook County, and raised on the west and south sides of the city. He spent much of his youth in public housing at Ogden Courts and the Henry Horner Homes. Although his family migrated to the Gage Park area in the late '70s, he returned to patrol the same streets of his childhood as a police officer for the Chicago Housing Authority Police Department in the 1990's.

Mr. Dukes received his education in Chicago's Public School system, and enlisted in the Marine Corps soon after graduation. After an Honorable Discharge from the military, he worked for the Veteran's Administration. However, after two years, he left the V.A. to become one of the second class of police officers for theCHAPD. During that time, he served as a Patrolman, Bike Officer, Youth Officer, and Investigator for Internal Inspections. Following the department's disbandment in 1999, Dukes moved to Black River Falls, Wisconsin, to become the Drug Enforcement Agent for the Ho Chunk Nation.

Upon leaving the Ho Chunk Nation, Dukes pursued higher education, and obtained a BA in technical communication, which opened opportunities for employment with 3M, the Marshfield Clinic, and UnitedHealthcare. He is currently retired and exploring artistic pursuits.

Mr. Dukes is the best person to author this story because he lived through it, and has the unique perspective of growing up as a resident of public housing, and later serving the community as a law enforcement officer.

Disclaimer

The following stories are a personal account of events from the author's point of view. Names have been changed or omitted to protect individual privacy or integrity. There is profanity and graphic content. Parental guidance is advised for readers aged 18 and younger. The information contained within is the author's intellectual property and cannot be used without his consent.

CHAPTER 1 – THE HISTORY OF CHICAGO'S PUBLIC HOUSING

Due to the Great Depression, there was a shortage of decent low-income housing. Plans for better public housing began to emerge in major metropolitan areas across America. Public housing arrived in the City of Chicago in 1937. From 1938 to 1976, these developments, often referred to as "projects," sprouted in various neighborhoods across the city and its local suburbs.

Initially, the structures were simple low rises resembling townhouses, seamlessly blending into the housing design of neighboring structures. Indistinguishable from other houses or apartments in the area, the lush green lawns were adorned with flowers and shade trees. Each unit was equipped with the latest appliances, making the new lodgings attractive both inside and out.

The waiting list for families interested in renting a unit was long, and the Chicago Housing Authority's, or (CHA), screening process was thorough. Applicants fortunate enough to be accepted as tenants gained easy access to public transportation, city parks, and schools. Later constructions were strategically located on prime property near the lakefront, and just miles from downtown Chicago.

The original residents of Chicago's public housing included the working class and World War II veterans, later joined by the unemployed and public aid recipients. All residents were required to sign a lease and adhere to the rules of the housing authority, strictly enforced with non-compliance leading to fines and/or eviction. Importantly, Housing's intent was not to permanently lease units but to provide functional, beautiful, and affordable short-term dwellings for veterans and their families. The idea was for residents to have respectable housing while they pursued further education or vocational skills to re-enter the workforce.

As the appeal of these dwellings grew, and more federal funds were invested, more developments were built. Inner-city areas underwent revitalization, and the new residents were no longer solely returning vets but also average citizens striving to get ahead. Further development led to the creation of housing for senior citizens, liberating Chicago's poor and working-class citizens from the challenges of dealing with slumlords and violent ghettos.

In the 1950s, high-rises became the new "projects." Rumors

suggest Windy City politics influenced the construction of multi-storied high-rise properties along the "black belts" of the city's South and Westside. The first high-rises comprised two to three-story buildings shadowed by a central seven to nine-story building, offering ten units per floor with one to three bedrooms and various amenities.

The newer developments housed more people per square block than any neighborhoods the city and county services had ever faced. Public housing's high-rises brought increased employment for various vocations to support housing and its functions, along with additional police and firefighters. Every conceivable support group was within walking distance, turning public housing into a utopia.

The final stages introduced super high-rises placed in the wastelands and roughest parts of the city, ranging from fifteen to twenty-two stories. The floor plans varied, but ten units per floor remained the norm. In addition to amenities from previous developments, the new high-rises included a laundry room on each floor or within the basement of some buildings. Public grammar and high schools, playgrounds, baseball diamonds, swimming pools, basketball, and tennis courts were all within walking distance, offering every detail and convenience for a quality standard of living at a fraction of the cost.

Over time, the demographics of public housing residents shifted, reflecting changes in the working class and racial diversity. As the ambitious working class of all races moved up and out, the generations that remained in public housing faced increasing challenges, resulting in a population that was poor, increasingly uneducated, and reliant on public aid.

Public aid and housing rules favored single women, leading to a shift in the demographic makeup of residents. Poor married and single men realized their families could have better shelter if they lived separately. Consequently, the greater percentage of legal residents within public housing became single females and their children, especially single Black women. This is where my story in Chicago's public housing began.

1969

My mother, Audrey Dukes, went to a branch office of the Chicago Housing Authority to apply for an apartment. My relatives had made their homes in buildings scattered across the Westside of Chicago. During her teens, my mother lived in the Lathrop Homes, while my great-aunt, and one of her daughters resided in the Henry Horner Homes. Another of her daughters lived in ABLA, near Maxwell Street—an area once known for blues musicians and Jewish merchants offering goods at affordable prices. We referred to the four-block stretch of real estate as "Jew Town."

That day, my mother visited an office building in the Harold Ickes Homes, taking me with her. This building was located on Cermak Road, adjacent to Clark Street and less than a mile away from Chicago's Chinatown. Within weeks, Momma's application was approved. Thirty-five years later, she recounted that day to me.

"Everyone was amazed at how quietly you sat with me and how patiently you waited." She said.

"I was about four years old, right?" I asked.

"I guess? What they didn't know was I'd get that ass if you clowned on me in public!" Momma joked.

I laughed at her remark, understanding the truth behind our chuckles. Despite her loving and doting nature, she would not have hesitated to discipline me or my siblings. Parenting was different then; they provided guidance, molding us into good and responsible individuals. It's my opinion, today's parents often seek friendship first, over discipline with their children, not realizing that respect precedes love. It was also a practiced protection to teach Black children how to act in the presence of White people, for fear that if you are too loud, or wild, that you might attract their attention and ire, which was and still is dangerous for us.

On a wintry night in late 1969, I was awakened by the bite of Chicago's bitter cold, often referred to as the "hawk." The frosty night air whipped at the bare skin between my pant legs and socks as my stepfather, Jake, carried me from the car into the building located at 2650 W. Ogden Avenue. To enter the lobby on the main level, my parents had to knock on the steel doors secured by a security officer who verified their right to be on the property. Once we were properly checked in, we rode the elevator to the top floor, and entered our new home in apartment 703.

All our belongings—bags of clothing, boxes, and furniture —were already arranged. I walked around the apartment, exploring spaces behind and beside the clutter. I fell asleep for the first time in the room that I would share with my brother for the next seven years.

CHAPTER 2 – YOUNGER DAYS

Welcome To The Ghetto

The first time my big sister and I were sent to the "Arab Store" for Momma, I was excited. I was happy to be going somewhere, anywhere, but we were in for a surprise.

It was cold out, so we were wearing our Eskimo coats! They were popular back then. The coat was made from polyester fabric with a fake fur lined hood that formed a tight tunnel that restricted your peripheral vision when zipped completely.

Mine was blue and hers was burgundy. I loved that coat!

As Momma handed Sister the grocery list, she looked at both of us and said,

"Be careful and cross at the light!"

"Okay!" I am sure we said in unison.

"And hold his hand!" I heard Momma say as we exited and slammed the door.

Down the flights of stairs, we ran, with me lagging behind Sister's long, eight-year-old legs. She was three years older than I was and tall for her age. I would not surpass her in height until I was 15 years old. We ran out of the stairway, through the lobby, and towards Ogden Ave. A few steps before the curb, Sister stopped to wait for me.

"Gimme yo hand," she said. I placed my hand in hers as we waited for the light to turn green.

Ogden had six lanes of traffic. There was a local lane on both sides of the street and four lanes in the center. The lights changed quickly, so we had to run as fast as we could across the middle. We were laughing as we made it to the far end, but that was about to change.

As we crossed the final local lane of traffic, two older boys started walking in our direction. I could feel Sister squeeze my hand tighter as we got closer to them.

"Uh-hey, uh, lemme git a quarter!" one said as we walked by them. The other boy cut around to the front of us and started grabbing at my sister's pockets.

I did not know what was happening, it was my first time being robbed, but I told them to leave her alone! Sister let go of my hand and was going around in circles trying to pull away from the boy who was trying to rob us. I grabbed the back of his coat and yelled at him again,

"Let her go!"

The other boy grabbed me by the hood of my Eskimo coat and punched me in the face. I fell backward to the sidewalk, crying and holding my eye and cheek. Sister rushed over to me with tears in her eyes and asked if I was okay. I could hear the boy's feet and laughter grow faint as they ran away from us. Welcome to the ghetto.

CAUGHT IN THE CROSSFIRE

Amidst the myriad challenges faced by those living and working within Chicago's public housing, the plight of the children was the most distressing. The well-maintained properties of my childhood visits were now a distant memory. In the twelve years between my last encounter with relatives still residing in the projects and my time patrolling the area as a police officer, Maintenance had long abandoned the battle.

During my family's residency, the Chicago Housing Authority

(CHA) mandated timely repairs and upkeep. Maintenance personnel, including mechanics and plumbers, ensured grass was cut, shrubs were trimmed, graffiti was painted over, and hallways and apartments maintained a fresh appearance. For children, maintenance promptly fixed or replaced broken swings, teeter-totters, or anything with moving parts.

Our playgrounds, constructed with concrete and steel, lacked thc plastics and childproof polymers seen in today's structures. Average children had little chance of damaging anything but themselves. I vividly recall a childhood incident when, at five years old, I was pushed off a six-foot-tall sliding board, landing headfirst on the concrete. Miraculously, neither my head nor the concrete suffered lasting damage. The primary threat to modern play areas comes from unruly teenagers.

Placed within view of residents' windows, the children's playground allowed parents to observe their children's activities. Baseball diamonds and basketball courts were a bit farther away, but pre-teens and young adults were trusted to venture out. Everything was thoughtfully designed for residents' convenience.

Initially, parents and relatives would sit on benches or stand along the fence, engaging in conversations while children played. However, as parents became less attentive, teenagers gradually took over the play areas. Violence was not new to the projects; even in the seventies, there was a gang presence in public housing. However, the roughnecks took the initiative to keep the fight away from where innocents might be.

The Vicelords ran Henry Horner, where my cousins lived, while the Goon Squad engaged in gang fights and shootouts with the police in Ogden Courts, where we lived. I was allowed to hang out with my cousin Wolf and his Vicelord friends. Considered a mascot, I was cute and cuddly, traits that came in handy with attracting girls, but also subject to teasing and being made to do things the bigger boys egged me into doing.

They called me "Walnut" because of my head's shape and size, while my cousin was called "Wolf" due to his unibrow, hairy arms, and visibly fine hair connecting sideburns to the hairline. Though four years older than I was, Wolf was the youngest of the pack, with the other boys ranging in age from 14 to 18 years old.

In those days, conflicts were settled with your hands, fists, or knives. The ethos dictated proving one's manhood or establishing a "pecking order." Fists, sticks, knives, and stones eventually gave way to bats, chains, and zip-guns, which were makeshift pistols crafted from car antennas. These crude weapons caused harm to both shooters and their targets.

My introduction to the street's brotherhood and its mentality occurred during these gang-related incidents. Everyone knew their neighbors, and the streets were particularly harsh on outsiders. Those in the know learned to avoid danger, and tried to look out for one another, if trouble arose. I was trusted to walk downstairs alone to go to the playground, if my cousins were already outside.

During weekends at Horner and stays at my great aunt's, I was always with the older boys, and they were always up to something. Small children were usually upstairs when the streetlights came on, or on their way to bed soon after dark. Entrusted to watch me, Wolf allowed me to hang out well past curfew. While the older boys engaged in various activities, I would be on the swings or repeatedly sliding down the slide at my leisure, as I was the only small child outside.

Late at night, while the older boys smoked and talked about local teenage girls, I was oblivious to the discussions. They would sneak sips of alcohol, pass around cigarettes, and I, the innocent mascot, had no idea about the adult matters they discussed.

One night, as I played on the swings, an older boy called out, "Walnut! Bring your little big-headed ass here!" As I ran over to them, they playfully grabbed my forehead, squeezing it, then passing me around. Treating my head like a basketball! They asked me to deliver messages to girls standing along the fence. I did as I was told without hesitation.

The teenagers often broke bottles and threw candy wrappers on the ground, and stayed out until early morning hours, laughing, playing, and breaking things. Maintenance would clean up glass, trash, spilled soda, and occasional puddles of urine the next day. However, good things seemed to come to an end. Time and personnel cutbacks affected the frequency of grounds and common area cleaning. The decline in proper home training, coupled with CHA's reluctance to evict problem tenants, contributed to trash accumulation in garbage rooms, stairwells, and other public areas. I am sure bigotry also played a role in the neglect and lack of responsibility to continue to keep public housing locations as neat and beautiful as they once were.

In my mother's era, tenants were fined for property damage and evicted for breaking housing rules. Those were the days when tenants used their own detergent, hot water, and brooms to clean the area in front of their doors. But those days were gone. Stairwells, once pristine, were now littered with garbage, human waste, and fluids. The galleries were stained and foul-smelling, turning the stairwells into filthy and dangerous spaces.

The garbage rooms were the most shocking, filled with unnecessarily large bags thrown into the room for the janitor to deal with. Super-sized bags meant for garbage chutes often spilled refuse on the floor. The garbage rooms became breeding grounds for large rats and roaches. Modern residents opted to throw their trash bags out of their apartment windows, leading to the sight of whole bags of garbage or soiled diapers plummeting from above.

The new generation of children played in a world of dirt and filth. While my friends and I were careful not to fall onto broken glass, these children trampled through millions of shards. They relied on their imagination and wits, sharing their concrete playground with older kids far more sinister than the teens I knew. In the nineties, swings were broken or missing, with only metal posts for benches, monkey bars, and sliding boards still standing. Nevertheless, the playground remained the congregation point for teens.

Project kids played tag, threw rocks at each other or at an overpopulation of pigeons, all while the teens observed. The children's laughter echoed in the dirty air, undisturbed by their surroundings, even gunfire.

The older siblings or parents of the playing children, the new teens, gathered strategically in the central play area.

It provided a perfect vantage point to observe police, drug customers, or rivals. Thugs had no qualms about using children for cover, knowing the police might hesitate to approach, if a child was present. They also believed opposing thugs might refrain from violence in the presence of a child, a belief often proven wrong.

Rap videos and Hollywood movies brought the harsh reality of drive-by shootings to the ghettos of Chicago. Gunshots would prompt children to drop to the ground, lying perfectly still until the danger passed. As the vehicle sped away and the dust and gun smoke cleared, the children would slowly rise, visually verify the danger had passed, and continue playing. Imagine that. The level of neglect and violence those children experienced daily could not prevent them from enjoying their playtime. Their moments to laugh together and dream because they refused to submit to fear. Play, pause, reset. Caught in the crossfire.

ONE LAST TIME

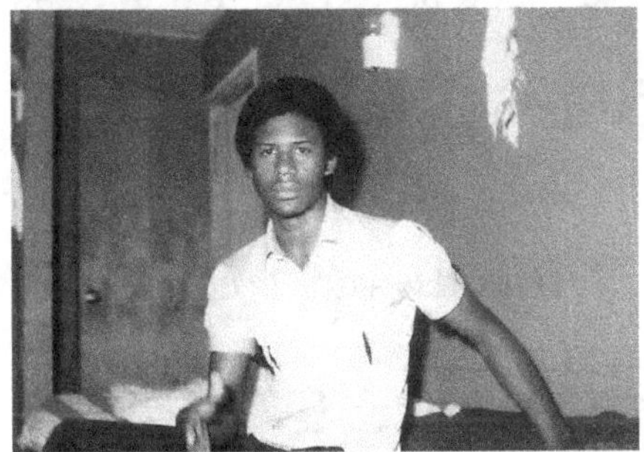

I revisited Ogden Courts and Henry Horner Homes a handful of times during my teens. Though most childhood friends had moved away, I managed to find a few familiar faces and secure safe passage.

K evin, my childhood friend fond of comic books, still retained his inner child. Bo the bully was serving time in juvenile hall, and my ex-girlfriend Laura was lost and turned out. I was told all about what happened to her in my absence from this place. I did not expect to see her, but I secretly hoped I would. How does the saying go, "When you least expect it, expect it!" It was unbelievable, but there she was, walking towards me.

Entering the building while my friends and I chatted in the breezeway, Laura's appearance struck a sharp contrast between her lithe, childlike frame and the heavy makeup, high-heeled boots, and coochie-cutter shorts she wore. My one-time girlfriend, there she stood, right in front of me. She was a "yellow gal," a "redbone," or "light skinned-ed" Her rabbit fur coat barely covered the plunging "V" of her halter top. She was just as beautiful as I remembered, and my 15-year-old heart pounded its applause at the sight of her.

With a cigarette in hand, she strolled over, and a silence fell over us all as she stopped and stood within arm's reach. Unsure of what to say, I could not stop staring at her face, hazel-colored eyes, and heavily glossed lips. I just smiled. Leaning back, she looked me up and down, crossing her arms and taking a drag from her cigarette.

"You're still a little boy," she remarked, exhaling smoke from the corner of her painted grimace.

The joyful expression on my face shattered, falling to my feet, drowned out by laughter from my friends and the silence of my lack of a comeback. Speechless, I could not fathom why she was trying to embarrass me. Perhaps she lashed out preemptively, but the reason behind her petty comment was a mystery to my juvenile mind.

Earlier, I had heard that she had a boyfriend, or rather a man friend. Some 30-year-old that had his own apartment in the "new buildings" or rather what we called the "nine stories." Her new love interest was said to have had kids by different women who lived in his building and the surrounding ones. He was a true "cocksman" or as we joked about guys like him, a "dicksmith!" These were the type of guys who did nothing but turn a woman's mind, heart, and privates inside out. It was the opposite of being "pussy whipped!" A cocksmans whipped that pussy!

It did not matter how many other women or children he had, his reputation in the streets kept them curious about what it was like to be with him, and his sexual prowess kept them coming back for more. These women would rather cuss each other out and physically harm one another, than complain to him about his behavior, or simply leave him alone. What chance does a pubescent girl have against a man that most adult females struggle to resist?

At 15, I was goofy, poor, and very much a virgin. I had no style, or game. I was exactly as she said, "a little boy." After all, she was a child having sex with an adult and most likely in the company of much older folks most of the time. She had an older brother, I forget his real name, but she called him "Doonie." I remember he was very protective of her. He liked my older sister and would allow Laura to tag along with him on his visits to see her. My friends did not know all the details about what happened to him, just that he died a victim of gun violence. Such a nice guy I recalled, murdered by gunfire. As beautiful as she was, I bet her brothers' rivals and plenty of hormonal males in the vicinity were itching for an opportunity to wrap her around themselves. My own friends were trying to take her from me all those years ago when we dated. Hooking up with Bo is what broke us up, but she has a man now. She's on to bigger and better things.

Her protector, like her innocence, was long gone. After she turned and walked away, I never saw her again.

SUMMER OF '83

Against my mother's wishes, I borrowed her boyfriend's car. With a week before going to the Marine boot camp in San Diego, California, I had time to have some fun after graduation. Five years earlier, my cousinWolf joined the Navy, returning to a war hero's welcome and as one of Henry Horner's most popular people. The Navy transformed him into a clean-cut young man, and he remained my childhood hero.

Returning to 141 N. Wolcott to share my departure news with Wolf and spend time with him and other male cousins was a must. Deciding to go get Wolf first and then head west to pick up Jay before visiting Jaime in Markham, I parked in front of the building, careful not to catch a flat tire on the broken glass. Faces on the porch looked as familiar to me as mine looked to them, surprisingly.

"Walnut? Oh, hell naw! He looks like a man! Walnut! That head though!" someone said with a snicker.

I tried not to laugh but could not help it. Most kids who hung out on the porch and allowed me to join them were still there. After hugs and dap, I inquired about Wolf.

"Any of y'all seen Wolf?" I asked.

"Oh, Wolf? Naw, man, I ain't seen 'em." One guy replied.

Noticing a slight chuckle from another, I did not make the connection initially. I told them I would be back and asked them to inform my cousin, if they saw him.

Jogging up the stairs to apartment 402, the scent of Pine Sol mingled with faint hints of urine, and the aroma of Aunt's fried chicken filled the air. As usual, the door was wide open.

"Oooh, I got here just in time!" I exclaimed as I rushed in.

"Hey, Pig!" Auntie greeted me as I rubbed my hands together and licked my lips.

"If you hungry, there's some in that bowl over there on the table." she offered.

"I only have time for one," I replied, picking a crispy wing from the steamy pile.

"Is Wolf here?"

"Uh-uh. He ain't in the back. I guess he's around somewhere." she said, focused on her skillet and crackling meat.

"I'm going into the Marines this Saturday, and I wanted to get with all the boys in the family." I proudly announced.

"Well, be good, Pig. Come see us when you get back," she said.

Grabbing another piece of chicken, I kissed her cheek and mumbled a goodbye through my greasy lips. Unbeknownst to me in the moment, it would be the last time I would see her alive, because she passed away several months later.

On her final day, Auntie heard the cries of a woman coming from the stairwell outside her door. She stepped closer to the door, recognizing it as her daughter's voice who lived in an apartment eleven stories above. My cousin, her daughter, was being beaten by her boyfriend, and she tried to intervene. However, the stress of the event led to Auntie suffering a massive heart attack. As she fell, her last words were, "I can't take this no more." Stepping over her, the abusive boyfriend continued his assault until other family members in the apartment intervened.

It is curious how often we interact without saying what needs

to be said, unsure, if it is our last chance.

Savoring the last greasy morsel of my chicken wing, as I exited

the building, I looked back at the fellows gathered on the porch

and walked towards the car.

"Hey, Walnut, here's Wolf!" someone called out.

Turning around, I scanned the crowd, not recognizing him

initially. Walking closer, I spotted him sitting on the bottom

step, looking skinny and unkempt. Laughter and chuckles

surrounded him, and my once hero had become a mere shell of

himself. The once young, handsome, popular, and witty young

man was gone. I did not know what kind of drugs he was on,

"syrup and pills" were pretty popular back then, but his lack of

hygiene and bloodshot eyes brought a lump to my throat.

"What the fuck is wrong with these guys? I thought they were

his friends." I pondered. I looked up to them. I thought we

were boys, that we were family. They looked pleased to see him brought so low and to see how life's defeat, and his downfall had registered on my face. Immediately, I was like, fuck them! They were nothing to me anymore. Wolf was my only concern.

His skin and clothing looked dusty, and his hair was unkempt and slightly matted. As I approached, he uttered something slightly incoherent, but I would not take no for an answer. I could not leave him there with these fools. I would not leave him.

"Come on, man. Roll with me. I don't know how to get to Patty's, and I wanted to hang out with y'all before I go into the service." I explained.

Pulling himself up, we walked to the car, drove over to picked up Jay, and then took a longer ride out to Markham to find my cousin Jaime. We walked around the neighborhood, drank beer, and reminisced. My world and the people around me were changing rapidly, but I was reaching for bigger and better things, or so I thought.

CHAPTER 3 – CHAPD THE CHICAGO HOUSING AUTHORITY POLICE DEPARTMENT

Community-Oriented Policing

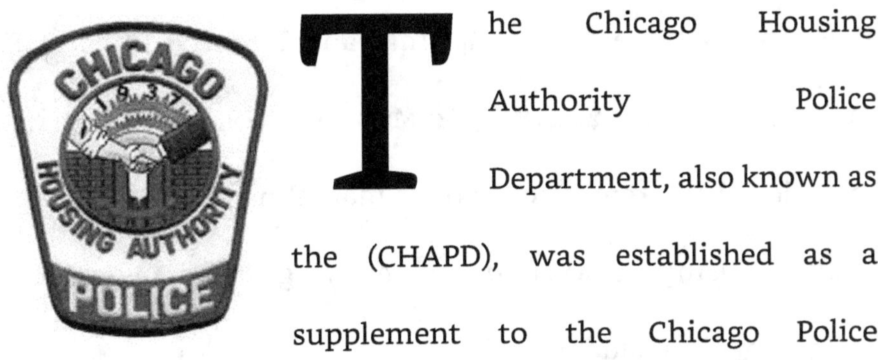

The Chicago Housing Authority Police Department, also known as the (CHAPD), was established as a supplement to the Chicago Police

Department (CPD), aiming to offer enhanced services for residents of one of the nation's most impoverished and crime-ridden low-income housing developments. It operated from October 30, 1989, to October 12, 1999.

The CHAPD achieved its daily objectives using "community-oriented policing techniques and aggressive vertical patrol" across all Chicago Housing Authority properties in the inner city of Chicago, Illinois, and some suburban areas under federal authority. Public housing, funded by federal and state sources, occupies two-thirds of Chicago's prime real estate and lakefront property.

The inception of the CHAPD was the brainchild of Chicagoan Vince Lane, who served as Chairman and Executive Director of the CHA from May 23, 1987, to May 26, 1995. In a television interview, Lane reminisced about marveling at the well-kept public housing as a child and envying the conveniences enjoyed by the residents.

During his tenure as Chairman, Lane took a personal stance to improve the safety and living conditions of residents by initiating the repair of dilapidated low and high-rise buildings, coupled with enhanced protective services for inhabitants.

However, realizing his vision was not without challenges. Lane's plan ran counter to the Mayor's Advisory Council report, published by the Chicago Tribune in July 1988, which proposed the demolition of 8,000 units of family high-rise buildings over a 10-year period.

Residents' complaints about the lack of police protection and the Chicago Police Department's (CPD) limited presence, along with documented concerns from CPD officers about the safety of patrolling public housing and responding to service calls, remained unaddressed by the mayor but were pivotal concerns for Lane.

Lane's solution to combat rampant gang-related drug sales

and crime was to establish a dedicated police department to work alongside the Chicago Police but with broader jurisdictional boundaries. Since public housing spanned various neighborhoods and local suburbs, the CHAPD was empowered to patrol federally owned property.

Before the CHAPD's creation, the federal government paid the City of Chicago $13 million annually for additional patrols to ensure adequate protection for CHA residents. CPD units were stationed at 365 W. Oak Street for Public Housing North and 4848 S. State Street for Public Housing South nearly twenty years prior to the CHAPD's inception. The CHAPD's initial station was at 4947 S. Federal Street within CPD's 2nd District, also known as the "Deuce."

Until the CHAPD was established, the CPD was responsible for providing police services to the majority of Cook County and the City of Chicago. Dating back to 1837, the Chicago Police Department is the largest police force in the Midwest and the second largest in the United States.

With 13,619 sworn officers and 2,625 other employees as of 2003, and 11,900 sworn officers and 948 civilian employees as of 2022, it is one of the oldest modern police agencies globally. However, it was deemed ineffective against the rising tide of violence in densely populated public housing by the local media and residents in Chicago's public housing in 1990.

CROSSROADS

At the age of twenty-three, my life stood at a crossroads. While I had the stability of a good government job, the trainee track I was on left me unsatisfied and bored. The role of an adjudicator, though purposeful, seemed to lack the excitement and challenge I craved. It did, however, offer a chance to serve my fellow veterans, a prospect that appealed to me deeply.

After leaving the Marine Corps with an Honorable Discharge,

I found myself living off my mother's support for three months before landing a job as a file clerk at the Department of Veterans Affairs. Yet, despite my best efforts to advance within the organization, I found myself hitting walls. Oddly, this occurred at a time when employers favored applicants with some college. Previously, a high school diploma was good enough for most entry level positions. There were still blue-collar employers who accepted non-H.S. graduates and or a general education diploma (GED). Persons in possession of an associate or a bachelor's degree were considered for management positions, but I had neither. Applications to other government agencies yielded no results, leaving me feeling stagnant in my prospects for financial growth.

The dream of furthering my education to nurture my artistic talents had always lingered in the back of my mind. However, I had convinced myself that school was a luxury I could not afford, especially after spending the last six years in the military. When you are young, four to six years seems like an eternity. I was also plagued with self-doubts about my ability to succeed, if I took a chance on higher education. It was time to work, not to dream! My time for playing was over.

My military service had begun with the noble goal of easing my mother's financial burdens and experiencing the world on my terms. At the age of 17, I had envisioned a future where I completed martial arts training in Japan, retired from the Marines at 38, and opened my own Dojo in Chicago to teach Karate for the rest of my days. Reality did not align with those plans. My military career ended after one enlistment, and I never served abroad as I had hoped.

The desire for a respectable occupation gnawed at me. Working endlessly among the files as a clerk held no appeal, and I found myself craving more. Yet, as much as I longed for change, I was uncertain of my readiness for new responsibilities. The confidence stemming from my military service clashed with the reality of being uneducated and lacking specific skills. I, like so many other poor and uneducated people bought into the propaganda that military service and the experience gained through it was enough to garner well-paying occupations upon returning to civilian life. I was young, delusional, and sorely disappointed.

In a bid to explore my artistic side, I began researching local art schools in downtown Chicago. Despite feeling ancient at the age of 24, in comparison to the younger 18 yr. old potential students who were also seeking admissions, during my interviews, I was accepted into the American Academy of Art. This was an exciting win for me, but soon enough, the strain of juggling school, work, and a relationship with my girlfriend began to wear on me.

Just as I was grappling with these conflicting desires, a new opportunity emerged. Months earlier, I had applied for a position in law enforcement, aiming to become a police officer with the Chicago Housing Authority Police Department (CHAPD). Though I was not selected for their initial class of officers, the CHAPD fulfilled their promise and contacted me by the end of summer. They informed me of a second class of officers scheduled to be admitted into the Timothy J. O'Connor Chicago Police Academy by the end of the year.

This news was a turning point. The job offered better pay, excellent benefits, and the stability I needed to buy a home and start a family. It seemed like the opportunity I had been waiting for, a chance to secure a promising future. Art school could wait; becoming a police officer was a chance to make a real difference in my life.

Excitedly, I rushed home to share the news with my mother, hoping for her support. However, her reaction was not what I had hoped or expected.

"Why in the hell would you want to do that?" she asked, her tone filled with anger.

My mother and I always had such a great rapport, I was always surprised when she was not in agreement with my choices, or appeared to be angry with me in situations where I did not perceive myself of "doing wrong." My attempts to explain and justify my decision fell on deaf ears. Her concerns about the risks and the lack of appreciation for law enforcement officers remained steadfast.

"People do not trust or respect the police. It makes no sense for you to risk your life for people who do not want your help!" she declared, her words cutting deep. I never doubted my mother's love for me. Her response, though tense, was one of concern. She was right about the sacrifices I made in enlisting in the Marines, could she be right about this too?

Though I understood her worries, I knew I had to follow my own path, even if it meant disagreement with those closest to me. My friend Reggie, shaped by his experiences with police brutality, echoed her sentiments, expressing vehement opposition to my career choice.

"So why in the fuck do you want to be pork? I'm sorry, man, but that's some bullshit. I hate the police, ain't never gon' like the police and muthafuck the police!" he exclaimed, his frustration palpable.

Sadly, like most men of color, and truth be told, poor White males also, I had my share of horrible encounters with Chicago Police Officers. I was with Reggie when a couple of Transit cops approached us on an EL train. We were teens at the time, 15 and 16 years old, respectively.

Both of us were into punk fashion, leather jackets, spiked bracelets, and such. He had a really cool bracelet that extended into the shape of a "V" across the back of his hand, which was exposed as we held the railings in the train car as it occasionally pitched from side to side. Interrupting our conversation, the cops immediately grabbed him by the arm and said, "You can't have this, it's a weapon!" As the first cop started pulling at it to remove it from Reggie's hand and wrist, his partner was struggling to hold my friend still as they wrestled with him. I was stunned.

Like everyone else in the car, I just watched. "My mother bought that for me!" he growled as he fought back tears and a cry in the back of his throat. The tall fat White cop who wrests it from him, opened the door in between the cars and said, "Well, she can buy you another one!" as he chucked it onto the tracks! I could tell Reggie wanted to do something to retaliate, but in the end, he stood there puffed up, embarrassed, angry, and defeated.

A few years later, while waiting for his food at a local Gyros spot across the street from my home, the police pulled up, entered the restaurant, and said Reggie "matched the description" of a robbery suspect and wanted to take him with them. Instead of complying, he bolted from the store, attempting to return to my house. He and a couple of my other neighborhood friends were hanging out in my basement. He got hungry and wanted to get food and return home before curfew. It was a school night.

My younger sister ran downstairs to tell us that Reggie was "fighting with the police!" We all ran out of the basement and out of the front door. I came outside and found eight officers tussling with him! My mother asked the officers what was going on, but they kept telling her to stay back! I tried telling them that he was my friend and that he just left our home, but they were not listening. Because Reggie was 6'1" tall and broad-shouldered as a kid, he always appeared older. He was strong as fuck too! At 14 years old, he was arm wrestling and easily defeating neighborhood adult males for money. Those cops could not handle him!

Finally, outnumbering him eight to one, they slammed him on the car! One short White officer climbed on his back to handcuff him. "Stop resisting! Stop resisting!" the cop yelled as he continuously pulled back on his wrists and the steel cuffs! "You're trying to break my hand!" Reggie screamed as his body and arm muscles tensed more to resist the officer's attack. It was at that time that Reggie's mom arrived.

I was accustomed to seeing her dressed professionally. She was always very well put together, but it was evident that she had been lying down for the evening because she was wearing a gown, housecoat, and her hair was wrapped in a scarf. Standing 5' 2" in her stocking feet, a stark contrast to her offspring, she quickly pushed through the crowd and cops to save her son. "What's going on? This is my child! Why are you all on top of him like this?" she demanded! "Get back now, ma'am, or you'll be in cuffs too!" the little White officer responded. "I wish you would put your hands on me! He is a juvenile! I am his mother! You will tell me what is going on right now!" she yelled. The cops quickly deescalated and explained why they stopped him.

It was at that time another unit arrived to tell the cops on the scene that they had the wrong person and could let Reggie go. The actual offender was in route to the district for processing. Reggie's mom said, "Yes, I need some badge numbers right now!" but they ignored her as they quickly scrambled to their vehicles to leave. Uncuffed, Reggie ran off into the night, ignoring his mother's calls to him. He was hurt and embarrassed again. He didn't want anyone to see him like that.

It did not matter, if the cop was Black or White, they never made me feel at ease, or as though they existed to keep me safe. The Black ones might have been apathetic, but the White ones, the White males were always angrier, intolerant, and itching for an excuse to get physical with you. I never dreamed that I would consider being a cop, but now that I was on the pathway, I was willing to give my all to it. I swore that I would never be like those cops. I was determined to be the absolute best I could be.

Even Tracy, my girlfriend at the time, surprised me with her reaction. Her disapproval was clear, and she issued an ultimatum: the job or our relationship. It wasn't unusual for me to seek the path of least resistance with her, but one of the biggest issues affecting our relationship was my earning potential. Previously, we got into an argument over how little I earned and my inability to pay rent or purchase my own vehicle. I was on the bus! I was making 11K to her 17K a year! She was calling me broke, but she was poverty-stricken too! To have this job, to work for the city would be life changing!

In that moment, I knew I had to choose the path that felt right for me, regardless of the fallout. So, I broke up with her. I decided that I could not stay with someone who was not supportive of me. She cried, I shook it off and kept it moving. Tracy, Reggie, and my mom were all reacting out of fear. I had my own fears, but I refused to let that dissuade me. I eased away from Reggie also. He was in a new relationship, a girl he met who lived out of state. Soon, he moved up to northern Wisconsin to be with her. It gave our friendship a chance to breathe, and I guess for he to miss hanging out with me.

Amid this turmoil and lack of support on all sides, Jason, my other childhood friend, and neighbor, received a similar letter from the CHAPD. His eagerness to join the academy mirrored my own, giving us a shared purpose and a newfound bond. His dad had been a cop, and he idolized that man. He had been on the waiting list for CPD for 3 or 4 years, as I recall. A ridiculous situation, I thought. No way I'd wait that long for anything, dismissing the fact that almost a year had elapsed since I applied and was denied acceptance into the first class of CHAPD.

As we both awaited our acceptance through the screening process, I reflected on the road that led me there. The decision was mine to make, and despite the doubts and opposition from everyone, my mind was set. It was time to forge ahead, even if it meant leaving behind familiar comforts and facing the unknown.

THE CHICAGO POLICE ACADEMY

The process of taking the written test and undergoing the psychological evaluation to become a police officer turned out to be easier than I had anticipated. The psychological exam mirrored the one I had taken before joining the Marines, with the requirement for applicants to answer yes or no to 100 questions. Here is a sample of the odd pattern of questions used:

Question: "I would like to be a florist."

Answer: "No."

Question: "I hate my father."

Answer: "No."

Question: "I am a special agent of the lord."

Answer: "No."

Though I found the test questions to be straightforward, many applicants did not. Surprisingly, statistics show that seasoned police officers, if they retake it, often failed this exam because of how much their experiences behind the badge change their perspectives. The physical exam and fitness test were also similar, though easier than what I had faced in the Corps. Gradually, I grew more at ease with the process, shedding my initial anxiety about the academy's curriculum and fears about graduation.

The three most eye-opening things that I learned from attending the Chicago Police Academy were my rights as an individual under the law, municipal code, and proper use of force. Ignorance and television clouded my knowledge and expectations in encounters with the police. Because the public is not versed on the law and their personal liberties, municipal code, or how police are trained to handle the various levels of contact and conflict with the public, the community being served is unaware of when they are being mistreated or are the victims of illegal conduct at the hands of law enforcement officials.

All of the laws written to protect our rights as an individual were put in place to prevent entities from abusing their power over us. However, there are so many laws in place to protect us, that it can be manipulated to make enforcement more difficult to catch those who are guilty. If proper steps are not followed in the execution of a search and or arrest, the case can be thrown out and the subject set free. Prosecution is even more difficult, if the subject can afford a good lawyer. Having money wins again.

With municipal code, littering, loitering, spitting, arguing, anything that can be a nuisance to the public and is capable of disrupting community norms are frequently ignored and go unenforced, unless you are part of the social underclass. Then they are used as a tool to justify detaining individuals or lead to an arrest at the officer's discretion.

Lastly, the use of force model, which is different across states, is generally used to determine the level of resistance and possible violence from a subject and the appropriate use of force to counter that resistance. Plainly, the officer can be a level above the threat. If you refuse to follow verbal commands, the officer can touch you to direct you. If you snatch away, passive resistance, he can apply pressure sensitive techniques to gain compliance. If you strike the officer, he can escalate to tear gas, a baton, or more physical techniques such as stunning you with fists. If all else fails and the subject uses a weapon or a tool that might cause injury or great bodily harm, the officer can move to using a handgun and applying deadly force. If you think about most incidents where a law enforcement officer used their weapon to injure or kill someone, it is rare that the offender or subject had escalated to the appropriate level for that force to be utilized.

As a cop, as a professional, we were taught that we were not allowed to use deadly force to get out of an ass kicking. We were cautioned that, if we did not enter a situation "on 10," we leave ourselves room to negotiate and deescalate. We cannot and should not spend an entire shift fighting with subjects. Officers should not shoot anyone who is running away unless they are a fleeing felon. A fleeing felon is defined as one who has just committed a heinous crime, such as rape or murder. If the offender is not stopped, they might commit similar crimes. The officer is expected to chase, wrestle, and cuff them.

We were also taught not to shoot at blind targets. Police are not supposed to shoot through doors, windows or into the darkness. If you cannot sight and accurately hit your target, you might harm an innocent person. Violence makes emotions run high. Fear and anger cloud judgement. Police officers are human and subject to frailty, but as trained professionals, it is they, not the public's job to control a situation and manage each accordingly. The most useful tool an officer has in the field is the brain and its ability to accurately assess a situation and decide the best action for an appropriate outcome. These lessons followed me throughout my career, and I have seen what happens to officers who strayed from their training.

Municipalities shell out millions of dollars for wrongful death lawsuits due to police misconduct and or overreach. Black men are often the victims of the "shoot first, ask questions later" mentality that was and is still applauded by many in law enforcement. These revelations and more left me conflicted.

Everything my mother warned me about, public perception of the police, my past experiences as a Black male growing up in Chicago, and watching my friends become the victims of police brutality gave me pause and what's more, a choice. Because of the "Blue Wall of Silence" and the underlying and pervasive "Good Ol' Boy Network," being a good cop with integrity was going to be a daily struggle. I thought that I could control and discipline myself, or that if I could avoid working with bad cops, I would be fine. Fate decided to test that theory.

Throughout our time at the academy, we were frequently visited by officers from the first class of our new department. One warning they emphasized repeatedly was that our job was no joke. Rumors swirled about the conditions of the projects, now transformed into a veritable war zone from the relatively peaceful neighborhoods I recalled from my childhood, thanks to the influx of drugs. Our academy instructors often told us that there were Chicago Police officers that have never had to draw their weapon on an offender in a 20 yr. career. The reason why was because of the district they worked in, or a position within the organization that took them off the streets. We, however, would be placed in situations where violence is an everyday escalated occurrence. We were "going into the shit!"

Among the first class of officers, there was one figure who stood out—Michael Richmond. In less than a year, he had been involved in multiple violent incidents, which resulted in him killing two offenders and maiming another in the line of duty. I remember seeing him for the first time in the gym at the academy. My classmates and I were practicing handcuffing techniques. Richmond, a white male in his late twenties, stood about my height of 5'11" but with a stockier build than mine. Back then, I would have compared him to the Ralph Kramden character of the 50's television show, The Honeymooners, but a more current pop reference would be the portly Peter Griffin from the adult cartoon, Family Guy.

I was amazed at how our instructors gathered around him,

fawning over him, and treating him like a rock star. As they hung on to his every word, my mind drifted. I imagined the scenes of violence he had encountered, watching him with a mix of curiosity and unease. Between answering their questions, I observed him biting deeply into a juicy red apple. This moment reminded me of a scene from the movie "Fright Night" where one of the central characters, Charlie Brewster, is watching in horror as his new neighbor, Jerry Dandridge, who also stood smiling as he devoured the juicy fruit within two bites. Charlie wondered, was Dandridge really a blood thirsty monster living among them in suburbia? In this instance, only Charlie was aware of the danger standing in their presence. This image of Richmond smirking struck a darkly humorous chord in my mind as I visualized him as the same, a bloodthirsty vampire. Time would show that my imagination wasn't far from the truth.

CHIEFS

The Chicago Housing Authority Police Department (CHAPD) had a succession of leaders from its inception in March 1989 until its disbandment in October 1999. The early chiefs included Gary Gunther, a retiree from the Illinois State Police, followed by Madren Anderson, the former District Commander for CPD's 2nd District.

Gunther and Anderson's tenures ended before the first class of police officers hit the streets. Following them was Ira Harris, who served as Chief until October 1991, during which CHAPD tragically lost its only officer in the line of duty.

Hosea (Hosey) Crossley succeeded Harris, serving from October 1991 to February 1994. With over twenty years of police experience, Crossley brought valuable insight into the challenges of patrolling public housing environments. Despite being respected by his subordinates, Crossley often clashed with the Local Advisory Council (LAC) over officer safety concerns.

Interim chiefs followed, including Joe P. Mayo and George Murray, each contributing to the department's development. Matthew Brandon, a CPD Patrolman with experience in Gang Crimes and PHS Tactical Teams, also served as Deputy and Interim Chief.

On December 1, 1996, LeRoy O'Shield assumed the role of the eighth Chief of Police for CHAPD. With thirty years of experience and a background in community-oriented policing, O'Shield was seen as a potential bridge for better cooperation between CHAPD. and CPD. However, his tenure did not unfold as expected.

Ultimately, LeRoy O'Shield and Harvey Radney were the last Chiefs appointed under the City of Chicago's direction.

CHICAGO HOUSING AUTHORITY POLICE DEPARTMENT ORGANIZATION

The Chicago Housing Authority Police Department (CHAPD) was divided into Operations Services, Administrative Services, Investigative Services, and the COPS Team. The department comprised five police districts—Robert Taylor, ABLA, Ida B. Wells, Altgeld Gardens, and Cabrini Green—each led by a Commander overseeing their respective stations.

Commanders reported to the Deputy Chief, who in turn reported to the Chief of Police. The Chief was subject to the authority of the Chairperson of Public Housing before the City of Chicago regained control in later years.

RANKS:

Chief of Police (Four Silver Five-Pointed Stars)

Deputy Chief (Three Silver Five-Pointed Stars)

Commander (Gold Oak Leaf)

Captain (Two Silver Bars)

Lieutenant, Inspector (One Silver Bar for Lieutenant)

Sergeant (Three Chevrons)

Corporal (Two Chevrons)

Police Officer (Assigned roles such as Patrol Specialist, Investigator, Gang Crime Specialist, COPS Team Member, Bike Patrol, ATV Unit Officer, K-9 Officer, Evidence and Recovered Property Section Officer, and basic Patrolman/Police Officer)

INVESTIGATIVE SERVICES:

The investigative functions fell under the Internal Inspections Unit. Organized crime was combated by members of the Narcotic and Gang Crimes Investigations, along with members of the Tactical units, Special Operations unit, DEA, and FBI task forces.

All CHAPD units coordinated their patrol efforts within the following CPD detective areas: Area 1 (Wentworth) and Area 2 (Calumet) covering the south and southwest sides, and Area 3 (Belmont), Area 4 (Harrison), and Area 5 (Grand Central) covering the north, west, and northwest sides of the city.

CHICAGO
1937
HOUSING AUTHORITY
POLICE

PATROL DIVISION:

The Patrol division included Vehicle and Foot Patrol, Patrol Specialists, COPS Team Members, Bike Patrol, ATV Unit Officers, Abandon Auto Unit, ERPS Officers, B.I.T.E., Canine Unit, and (prior to its demise) the Warrant Unit.

DEMOGRAPHICS:

Male: 92%

Female: 8%

White: 16%

African American/Black: 80%

Hispanic: 3%

Asian: 1%

COMMUNITY ORIENTED POLICING STRATEGY (COPS):

The CHAPD pioneered community policing techniques in Chicago through their Community Oriented Policing Strategy (COPS) program in public housing, years before the Chicago Police Department's Chicago Alternative Policing Strategy (CAPS) program. The COPS Team was created as a special unit to establish rapport with public housing residents that regular patrol units could not.

Given the unique building designs and population density, CHAPD's COPS Team engaged with the community daily, aiming to instill a constant sense of security. They participated in sporting programs, after-school events, and built relationships beyond law enforcement interactions. Bicycles and All-Terrain Vehicles (ATVs) were utilized for close contact, allowing officers to foster relationships and gather information to deter crimes.

The COPS Team regularly attended CPD Beat Community Meetings, making officers more approachable when community members needed help.

The "Real" Police?

The CHAPD faced public confusion about its legitimacy, often being mistaken for a security force due to the CHA's history of employing contract security firms. The media further contributed to this confusion by referring to CHAPD officers as a "security force" rather than "police officers."

The department began with a single police station in Robert Taylor Homes. The first class of 86 males and five females underwent training at the Timothy J. O'Connor Chicago Police Academy as state-certified Peace Officers. While following a curriculum similar to CPD recruits, CHAPD recruits underwent intensified physical fitness and combat training due to the nature of public housing environments.

SALARIES:

Starting salary for CHAPD officers was $19,104, increasing to $49,723 over eight years, making them the highest-paid police officers in Chicago until the department's dissolution in 1999. This higher salary often caused tension with CPD officers but also proved beneficial when the Fraternal Order of Police union negotiated higher salaries for CPD with the City of Chicago.

As of now, starting salaries for CPD officers are $43,104, rising to $55,723 after one year, and further increasing to $58,896 after 18 months.

THE POWER OF LIFE AND DEATH

Our combat training team and range masters approached the danger and our preparedness with utmost seriousness. Officer Marsh, renowned for his Use of Force model adopted by CPD and other law enforcement agencies nationwide, was often called upon to testify in court on its proper application.

Interestingly, Marsh and a select group of officers at the academy preferred carrying knives over guns for their off-duty weapons. The idea of opting for cutting-edge weapons over the blunt force of handguns chilled me, suggesting their welcome readiness to engage up close and personal with possible offenders during off duty encounters.

We, however, received no knife training. Instead, on the range, we delved into various aspects of officer safety, including weapon maintenance and retention. One video that particularly struck me displayed the terrifying speed and skill of a man wielding a blade, showcasing the vulnerability of an officer in such a situation. It offered a glimpse into why they favored knives.

The first time I held my service revolver, an odd sensation washed over me. The chrome-plated steel felt weighty in my grip, and the realization dawned on me—I held the power of life and death in the palm of my hand. It was a sobering responsibility that left me cold and nervous. While I was trained to expertly shoot an M16-A1 rifle at ranges beyond its designed capabilities, I had never faced combat, and live ammo was strictly prohibited for enlisted personnel, even during fire watch. I fired a 45 cal. during basic training, but that was the only time I ever held any handgun.

Unlike other departments that allowed automatic and semi-automatic handguns, we carried revolvers with a mere six-round capacity. The benefit of a "semi" was the extra ammo per clip, providing a tactical advantage in certain situations.

The range instructor emphasized a critical point: accuracy over quantity.

"If all you gonna do is spit lead, then just take the rounds out and throw 'em! Just chuck 'em at the offender! You're wastin' 'em anyway!" Our Range Instructor quipped.

The actual training to fire the weapon was weeks away, with the authorization to carry coming months down the line. Would I be mentally and emotionally prepared when the moment arrived to use it?

Another influential figure in our physical conditioning was Gus Tero. He was a member of a family of brothers who all served the city as firefighters, but he chose policing. He was also the brother of the famous television and movie star Mister "T." Tero stood out at 6' 4" and well over 250 pounds. He was a powerhouse of fitness, and three times a week, he put us through our paces with exercises and lengthy runs. Multiple classes of recruits trained by him every day and he did almost every exercise with you! He was insane! Sometimes for the fun of it, he'd have us run the staircases of a local parking structure before our run back to the academy. He was watching, waiting until we were all looking ragged and tired before bringing us there. He would also run you straight towards the academy, then turn within a block of it to dash any hopes you had for the torture to end! Fortunately, my nightly five-mile runs kept me in stride. Two classmates of mine, fellow Marines, often led the pack. We pushed each other to excel.

In no time at all, 24 weeks had slipped by, and we found ourselves preparing for the state exam and graduation. Each classroom banded together, assisting classmates with study sessions, and ensuring fitness levels were maintained.

A week before graduation, some senior officers took us on a field trip to the areas we would be entrusted to patrol. WOOOO-BABY, it was on and popping! Literally! Loaded into yellow school buses, we were driven around the city to various locations to observe vice in action in its natural habitat. As we drove southward down the fire lane of the Robert Taylor Homes, we approached what was called "The Hole." Our senior officer was calling out the locations and activity to us when the POP, POP, POP started!

Someone shot at the busses in our caravan! It started raining gunfire! Like the crescendo in a symphony, the volume grew! He told us to get down as he crouched, as calls went out to dispatch of "shots fired at the PO-lice! 10-1! 10-1! Mickey

Caldwell's Cobra Stones, known as MC's, followers of the philosophy under the five-point star of the Black P. Stone Nation were saying hello and sending us a message. "We are not afraid of you!"

As we quickly exited the area, taking a quick right onto Garfield Boulevard towards the expressway and back to the academy, there were nervous chuckles and a few concerned faces. I felt that we had just experienced everything we needed to know about what awaited us once we went into full uniform and hit the streets. Bring it on!

Sadly, we lost two officers during the training period. Jason, my childhood friend that I started this venture into law enforcement with, was approached by the city to join CPD, they called his number while still at the academy. Another officer from a sister group in the academy, fractured her ankle during the final physical agility test, disqualifying her from completing the training. Jason went on to climb the ranks and successfully fulfil his dreams with the city, and the other cadet also found employment with the city as a Dispatcher.

As our graduation day neared, the rest of our class was divided among the three new CHAPD stations and the original station at the CHAPD in Robert Taylor Homes. We stood on the threshold of our new roles, armed with training, camaraderie, and a sobering awareness of the power we held in our hands.

BOSSES

Our initial leadership members were retired Chicago Police Officers. Some had achieved the rank of sergeant or had experience in investigative services, such as evidence and recovered property (ERPS), dispatch, area detectives, or youth officers. All of them received higher rank and pay for being the brain trust of this fledgling department. Overall, and in my opinion, we received the best people for the job. Working in CPD's system required individuals that knew it intimately, and also were well established in their reputation before leaving the city. That allowed them to gain cooperation from Watch Commanders and other CPD district personnel, who felt it was their jobs and sole purpose to frustrate us at every turn.

Seriously, there were countless times where I came into a district station with an arrestee in custody, ready for processing, and my paperwork was refused, or I was made to wait an unusual amount of time before my offender could be taken into lockup. Our supervisors were often called to appear at the district to have a conversation with CPD about the games that they would play with us while processing an arrestee into their system. There are few things more embarrassing to me than the times that I had a desk sergeant screaming and me in front of my prisoner about how I should have drafted my paper, or because they questioned the charge that I had given the individual. It was inappropriate and highly unprofessional, but the constant micro and macro aggressions shown towards us was a huge part of the initial reason so many people did not take our department seriously at first. We were constantly being undermined by the rank and staff of CPD.

Our bosses were true professionals and showed up for us while we were on patrol and when we needed someone of authority to push back on the districts or fight our battles. However, when the shift was done, when it was time to go home after a long day in the projects, they left their CHAPD stars and credentials in their lockers at the station. It was the Chicago Police star that they carried off duty and the coveted checker headband that hung from the rear-view mirrors of their personally owned vehicle, (POV). It was the CPD badge and identification that they had in their wallet, or looped over their belt and on their hip. If by chance they were stopped by another Chicago Police Officer or had to take a police action while off duty, this is what they wanted to be seen.

This angered and disappointed a lot of the officers I knew. It was a betrayal of sorts. Yes, they earned their CPD credentials and their retired status, but if the CHAPD was really "the Real Police" why not wear the symbol of the new department? Why not show your subordinates how proud you are of them and display a sense of allegiance? Nope. It was obviously more important to them that those outside of the realm of the projects know that they were "one of them." Not one of us, but one of them. Whether it was a weakness of character, or common sense, that was how it was, and how they rolled.

The rank of corporal (Cpl.) was not new to me. It was my final rank before leaving the Corps. In a police setting, it was the rank of our full-time trainers who also assisted in the field as a sergeant would. Not all field training officers (F.T.O.s) were Cpl. and vice versa. They were first in line for the rank of sergeant, but the few we had did not want the rank or responsibility, retaining their status until their tenure on the department was done.

As the department continued to grow, so did our leadership. Through lateral transfers and promotions, we were becoming "top heavy." The word was out! The department was viable and there was ample opportunity for promotion. Our salaries rivaled or exceeded most departments, including CPD. Suburban cops were applying for leadership position and were coming aboard. Most were uninterested in working for the city, because of its residency clause, but that was not a requirement to work in public housing. They could keep their home and continue to live in a "quiet" suburban community, while making a metropolitan salary. Funny thing, the suburban laterals had no problem with giving up their stars and badges from their local townships to wear ours. A huge contrast in comparison to the leaders with connections to CPD.

However, unlike the ex CPD bosses, the laterals were more difficult to find on the radio, or to stumble across in the field. We were often too busy to be jacking around, but it was not surprising to be sitting near a location and have a boss roll by. The HUD Chairman, Vince Lane was known to show up at all hours, days, or evenings, and walk through the buildings citywide. If he noticed activity, he'd call it in.

Once, while leaving a domestic dispute at an address, we crossed paths. As the elevator door opened before my stop, Chairman Lane and his security detail stepped on. It was impressive! I learned to lead by example from my boot camp Drill Instructors and throughout my military career. To see this creed, this concept in action filled me with pride. It was such a dangerous time in the city, especially in public housing, but there he was, our senior leader, out in them streets! Not so much for the laterals!

It was very obvious that some of them were accustomed to being neither seen nor heard during their 8 hr. shifts. Maybe that was the way it was done in smaller towns? They did their tour and turned over the functions to the next watch, collected their check and went home at the end of the day. That was their norm.

As the 90's grinded to a close, politics began to change, and the old ideas began to re-emerge in regard to the future of public housing as something new again.

Looking back on our history and the department's inception, we were doomed from the start. The residents, the structures where they dwelled, and where we actively patrolled were doomed from the very beginning.

The Black residents were never wanted as tenants, but federal fair housing laws intervened. Allowing them to move in became an easier pill to swallow by the first Mayor Daley as a concentrated voter base, in exchange for the privilege of residency. The structures were well built, but poorly maintained for decades. They were also on prime real estate with locations along the lake front, Chinatown and with unobstructed views of the skyline. Devising a means of disbursing the residents legally was underway under the guise of health and comfort.

The residents could have been better tenants, but the authority had long given up on repairing the apartments, common areas, and general maintenance of the grounds. Lane, while it was under his care, did what he could to bring the projects back to life, molding them once again into a place that was clean, beautiful, and safe.

One of the last big projects he undertook was to gut all of the dilapidated apartments in buildings across the city and rebuild them from the floor up. New paint, tile, plumbing, appliances and wider doors and ramps for better handicap access! This was an easier task in the older buildings due to the cinderblock walls, but in newer structures with drywall, they were repaired also.

Lane installed modern playgrounds for the children, replacing the concrete and steel I played on with plastics and foam surfaces to prevent the little ones from unnecessary scrapes and falls. New sod was laid where the grass was worn and missing. Even the elevators were replaced or received a facelift. The swimming pools and tennis courts were not revived. Most of the pools were cemented over in the 60's, due to cost, staffing, and the dread felt by White people over the possibility of sharing a pool with negroes. Only the baseball diamonds and basketball courts remained for the teens.

Public perceptions of blight and the bigotry associated with the assumption of tax money wasted on handouts for Black folks made it an easier sell to the general public that the masses of poor people in public housing would be better served by receiving rent vouchers and relocated to local suburbs where they might also enjoy living in a "quiet community" with better access to jobs.

Some communities were interested in the federal dollars and the guarantee of monthly rent received like clockwork, but they were in for a rude awakening. After generations of poor living habits and differing cultural norms, the welfare tenants were difficult tenants. The loud music, littering, fighting, domestic disputes, and drug dealing were transferred, introduced, and injected into these areas on a scale that those first communities were utterly unprepared for.

It's not that White folks are somehow inherently too good for criminal activity and are incapable of being destructive. We had plenty of dusty toothless White drug dealing gangbangers in the city, but they were in smaller numbers. When the senior Daley was mayor, and public housing was placed in his neighborhood stronghold of Bridgeport, he snapped! Place the buildings in the blighted locations, or the "Black belts," but not there! Therefore, when the projects suited their purpose, assisting tenants to live affordably, until they could move on, most White families moved out, bought homes, or moved into an apartment in all White neighborhoods.

The truly poor and working-class White neighborhoods in the city had a culture built upon the premise of being "better" than Black and Brown people." Anything negative that you could do as a person, or group was blatantly called "nigger shit!" Not "nigga" or "ghetto," as they are used today, but "nigger shit." The shame and stigma of that moniker in Chicago's Irish dominated, Italian, Polish and Lithuanian tolerated town, kept these areas immaculate. Their houses and apartment buildings looked like wooden shacks, and the vehicles on the block were seldom new, or fancy foreign makes, but their streets were free of litter and potholes. No one stood on the corner, and it was rare to hear someone driving by blaring their music.

Until I was able to get out of my community and see more of the country, I use to believe a lot of this, and accepted it as how some Black people chose to live. After seeing the trailer homes, or a double-wide for the "baller-billies," with a new "dually "4x4" pickup truck, and a nice Harley motorcycle out front, but with newspaper on broken windows or bedsheets for shades, I realized that it was more of a poor people thing than a "Black thing." Being broke influences some poor folk to overextend themselves to buy toys, and make noise in order to be seen, instead of investing in basic creature comforts or to be considerate of others.

The suburbs and rural areas that were able to steer clear of their riff raff by keeping them corralled in the trailer courts and out of the more upscale neighborhoods, did not anticipate what was to come. Most, if not their parents, left the city and consigned themselves to a two-and-a-half-hour ride or less in traffic twice daily to escape the city's taxes and of course minority population. They were able to shun and make fun of their rednecks, hillbillies, hippies, and crystal meth heads, but the new community of project folks were going to put their sensibilities to the test.

Lastly, the CHAPD was created as a supplement to CPD to do a better job of providing frontline services to a neglected populace was unwanted. We were an unexpected rival that was given millions of dollars that were originally earmarked for the city and CPD. We through hard work and diligence reduced crime across the city by containing the violence and drug dealing within our areas of patrol. That accomplishment reduced the fear the city had in getting rid of us when politics changed.

The city and our new leadership, the CPD Transition Team, wasted no time and took every opportunity to tell the residents of Chicago and anyone within viewing range that we were not really the police. Over and over again, we were referred to as a "security force." It seemed harmless at first, but when the Transition Team actively started to dismantle us and pull us from the streets to answer calls for service, no one complained but us. When the city decided laying us off was an option, there was no public outcry. The residents who grew to love us, because we were theirs and we always came running to their assistance, were being disbursed to the various suburbs, or set out on the street to fend for themselves. The general public had no stake in our future, but I believe that if they knew the city was planning to lay off over 600 law enforcement officers, there would have been more concern. I was surprised at how little the ACLU, and the NAACP did to save our jobs, but more about that later.

CHAPTER 4 –
REAL STORIES OF
THE CHAPD

Precursor

Excitement and anticipation coursed through us as we eagerly awaited our chance to hit the streets and become the "po-lice." The very idea of patrolling, of being the guardians of order and safety, filled us with a sense of purpose and pride. We were ready to step into the role we had trained so hard for, and we intended to be effective in the communities we were sworn to protect.

However, our ambitious plans were abruptly halted, if only for a moment.

The housing authority, facing budget constraints, couldn't immediately provide us with the essential gear we needed: body armor. This realization was a sobering reminder of the stark realities of the environments we were set to enter. The projects, known for their dangers and challenges, required us to be fully equipped for the tasks at hand. Without the proper protection, venturing into these areas was simply out of the question.

Yet, we weren't about to sit idly by, waiting for the funds to materialize. We were eager to get started, to have influence, and so we found ourselves posted at the senior citizens' buildings. Here, we listened intently to the calls for service echoing from the beats within our designated patrol area.

The mix of emotions within me was undeniable—a blend of exhilaration and caution. Excitement bubbled within as I imagined the scenes playing out on the streets, the unknown officers responding to dispatched calls with unwavering determination. Their voices, projecting strength, professionalism, and authority, echoed in my mind.

Each call, each situation they encountered, seemed like a challenge they were more than capable of handling. It was both inspiring and daunting. I longed for my turn, for the moment when I would step into that role, ready to face whatever came our way.

Every passing moment felt like an eternity, filled with the anticipation of the unknown. I could hardly contain the eagerness building within me, the burning desire to prove myself in the field. Soon enough, I knew, our chance would come. And when it did, I was determined to meet it with all the readiness and resolve I could muster.

FIRST NIGHT ON THE JOB

As luck would have it, I always seem to draw the shortest straw. Following the graduation ceremony, each of us received the name of our field training officer, duty station, and Watch assignments. And, true to form, I got everything I didn't want: the Robert Taylor Station, midnight shifts, and Michael Richmond—known as "the Vampire."

I made an effort to arrive at work early, but somehow managed to show up with only fifteen minutes to spare. Before I left for my first night of patrol, I sat and talked with Momma and the family.

There was a mix of fear and pride in Momma's eyes—a stark contrast to the beaming pride she had shown at the graduation ceremony. Their hugs and good luck wishes were worth being a few minutes late for.

In the Corps, we learned that it takes about 12-15 minutes for your eyes to adjust to the darkness and gain night vision. However, the streetlights and vehicle headlights hindered my pupils from fully dilating. As I arrived at the station, I could barely make out the outlines of things in the darkness outside the buildings.

Walking into the station parking lot, I greeted a few of the senior officers who were checking their vehicles or heading out for the day. They didn't seem particularly friendly or welcoming, which was a bit disheartening. I had hoped for a warmer reception, but I figured maybe the first-class officers were saving their embraces for those who survived the night, let alone the probationary period.

Entering through the rear entrance, which doubled as a lockup area and break room, I approached the desk officers. I received the same treatment, along with some brief directions to the roll call room.

Stepping out of the front door of the station into the breezeway, I quickly glanced over my shoulder out into the playground before heading into the stairwell.

The stairs felt slightly gritty beneath my shoes with each step, and the familiar scent of Pine Sol mixed with a faint hint of urine greeted me. It was the unmistakable scent of home—the "jets," as we called it. Exiting the stairs onto the second floor, I opened the door in front of me, only to realize I had walked into Dispatch. I was swiftly ushered back out onto the gallery, where I found the door to the left leading to the roll call room.

Inside, the other officers were already seated, and I realized I was the only one running late. Richmond stood at the rear, casually eating an apple as he leaned against the wall. The watch commander, entered and called for attention to roll call.

The Sergeant, though appearing to be in his mid- to late fifties, exuded a sense of authority, fitness and experience that commanded respect. He went through the numbers: arrests made, types of crimes committed, names of wanted offenders, homicides, and shots fired calls from the previous watch. Meanwhile, the distant sound of gunfire echoed in the night air.

Just as the roll call seemed to be winding down, one of the dispatchers entered to summon Richmond into their domain. He quickly returned and informed the Sergeant that he and his probationary officers were to respond to a call next door—a report of men with guns.

The excitement and tension in the room were palpable as we all prepared to head out into the night, ready to face whatever challenges awaited us on our first shift on the job. The adrenaline was pumping, and I couldn't help but feel a surge of nervous energy mixed with determination. This was it—the moment I had been waiting for, the beginning of my journey as

a police officer.

4853 S. FEDERAL

My heart thumped in my chest as I walked up the fire lane with my FTO and fellow PPOs to the location of our call at 4853 S. Federal. The scene was bustling with people, each corner illuminated by the dim, amber glow of the few remaining light bulbs. Denise and Dave were headed towards the elevator when Mike called out to them.

"Hey guys, this way," Richmond said, a toothpick sticking out of the corner of his pursed lips. He paused, casting a glance over his shoulder before leading us into the stairwell.

As we ascended the cluttered landings, he spoke up, his voice echoing in the narrow space.

"We don't take the elevator. They piss, shoot, and throw things down the elevator shaft. If they open the doors, you're trapped until someone lets you out. Don't be lazy. Taking the stairs may save your life."

Finally, we reached the 16th floor. My thighs were tight but not throbbing, and the smell of gunpowder lingered in the air. People milled about on the gallery, witnesses to what had occurred, yet I knew no one would speak up.

"2821 squad," Richmond called out.

"Go ahead, 21."

"Yeah, give us a 19 Paul, and we're clear," Richmond replied.

The dispatcher responded promptly, "Good 21, you can take the man down at 4342 S. State."

"We're on it, squad. Mobile out. Let's go, you guys."

We hurried back to the station parking lot to retrieve our vehicle and respond to the new call. As we made our way down the stairs and out of the building, I heard voices echoing our location.

"Robo's on the stairs! Robo's on 16! Robo's on the lane!"

It was reminiscent of the Marine Corps' fifth general order—to repeat all calls more distant from the guardhouse than my own.

With our squad's lights flashing and the siren blaring, we zoomed down State St. This was real—the sights, sounds, and smells were becoming familiar, imprinting on my senses. Blindfolded, I'd recognize this place by the scents and sounds alone.

Arriving at the scene, we found that the "man down" was a boy, a 13-year-old male with a gunshot wound to his lower right thigh. Chicago Fire Department ambulance number 18 was already on the scene, transporting him to Provident Hospital. CPD and a few of our units were present, working to disperse the crowd. Mike relayed the information, giving it a code for dispatch.

It was a hot night, not due to the temperature, but the constant calls for service. We'd receive shots fired calls every two to three times an hour, making the night crackle with tension. "Homey" loved to "bust a cap," with youth cutting holes in the wrought iron fences or firing shots from apartment windows.

Back in the vehicle, my senses were overwhelmed. Residents, children, drifters, winos, and hypes filled the streets at all hours. Past midnight, the activity rivaled daytime. Neon signs flashed out of sync, mingling with scents of Bar-B-Q, dust, fried chicken, and the new vehicle upholstery that distracted me from my FTO's instructions.

"Guys, ya gotta get your radio ears. You need to always be aware of where the other beats are, and the type of call dispatch gave them. They may call a 10-1, and in the confusion, you can't hear what they are saying to dispatch," Mike emphasized.

Almost on cue, a unit requested backup at the Harold Ickes Homes, north of our beat.

"2831 is going!"

"...32 is in!"

"Put 2842 in route, squad." Every available unit was rolling for the assist—a tradition passed down from the first class.

We raced up and down State and Federal, assisting units and receiving our on-the-job training. Mike pulled the vehicle onto the fire lane and switched off the headlights. It was pitch black—most porch lights were out, and only a few distant streetlights flickered on.

"Uh, Richmond, why are we rolling with no headlights?" I asked.

Before he could respond, the cracking sound of gunfire and the shattering of our light bar answered for him.

"Fuck! That's why!" Richmond yelled, hitting the gas as we sped through broken glass and gravel.

"Where are we going, man?" I shouted.

"We're gonna go back and get those motherfuckers!" He replied, cutting across the sidewalk and swiftly off the curb.

Parking on the Federal side of the building, Richmond urged us to lock up the vehicle as he jogged towards the darkened breezeway, weapon drawn.

"Put us out of the vehicle on a premise check at 4545 S. Federal, Squad," Mike instructed.

"Building check at 4545. 10-4, unit," the dispatcher confirmed.

Like baby chicks following our mother goose, we filed into the building's rear.

4545 S. Federal was a mix of vacant and occupied units. The lobby was empty, dimly lit, and eerily silent. Mike lowered the volume on his radio, and we followed suit. With our Maglite beams leading the way, we ascended to the 9th floor, peering into vacant apartments along the way.

CHA Police officers were required to do two building/premise checks per beat during regular patrol. These checks served as a record of open units that could pose hazards to residents or attract drug dealers and the homeless. They also ensured officers were present, giving residents a sense of security.

Mike led us into apartment 1605, where we found spent casings near the windows. Although we hadn't located the exact apartment the shots came from, it was clear this unit was being used by gang members for indiscriminate gunfire. Mike quickly noted the details in his notebook and called it in, assigning a code to the call for dispatch.

We ended the evening with more patrol, while waiting for calls for service. About an hour before the end of our shift, we stopped at a greasy spoon for breakfast. Once the food was served to us, Richmond called dispatch to request lunch. It was always best to wait until your meal was ready, because you never knew if you'd have to run to a job, or lend an assist. Thirty minutes to eat, another 10 to return to our sector brought us within 15 minutes of our time to return to the station and end our shift.

LET'S GET OUR HANDS DIRTY

Every FTO had a specialty. Some had more than one. Some liked to find dope and chase drug dealers. Some of the trainers loved searching for guns, where they were stashed and pulling them off offenders. Our FTO had one passion, or so it seemed. He loved to get guns! He wanted to be anywhere and everywhere that there were shots fired. Because of the environment we worked in, we constantly had hot calls for service. Hot calls were domestic disturbances, men selling drugs, men with guns, and shots fired!

On a rare occasion we processed a sexual assault. Another rarity involved crimes against children or neglect. I remember one night while looking for a shooter in "the Hole," We stumbled across a toddler. She was a three-year-old that was wandering around by herself at 2 am. Dave Chappelle made a joke about a Baby wandering around in the ghetto. My story occurred almost 20 years earlier.

She was nonverbal, but she was obviously very bright. We called her in to dispatch and tried to help her retrace her steps. As we were walking down the first building to help her find her parents, a sibling found us in the stairwell on the third floor. The baby released my hand and reached for her brother. He said that they had just moved to an upper apartment and that she must have taken a spoon to open the door. After going on her adventure, she probably didn't remember that the old apartment wasn't home anymore. I thought, "well duh! She's a baby!" We took some information for an Incident Report and returned to patrol.

Another night, at the beginning of third shift, Richmond saw a guy playing basketball. He walked over to him, grabbed him, and put him on the ground.

"What are you doin' man?" the subject asked angrily.

"Oh, you thought I forgot, that I wouldn't see or find you?" Mike said.

"2821 squad! Give me one for coming into the station for rock cocaine." Richmond called.

"One for POC in the station, 10-4, 2821." Replied dispatch.

The subject started trying to pull away from Richmond, saying, "I ain't have no drugs on me! Folks! Folks! They trying to take me to jail Folks!

After completely cuffing him, Richmond pushed the offender

face down in front of us as we heard an odd and thunderous sound. The subject's call for his FOLKS was the Black Disciples that lived in his cluster of buildings that surrounded us outside of 4848 and 4900 South State Street. The sound was coming from all of the people who were running down the stairs to come to his rescue and prevent his arrest. Richmond called a 10-1 at our location and drew his baton.

We circled our prisoner on the ground and stood shoulder to shoulder with our backs toward each other and our faces towards the crowd.

Mike said, "Stand your fucking ground guys!" as the masses descended upon us growing closer with each step! Before the crowd could close on us and box us in, I saw CPD's blue and whites climbing the curb with lights and sirens blaring! Every officer in the station that was free came running up the fire lane! Public Housing South Officers did something I had not seen until this point, take a police action! Everyone not wearing a blue shirt got their asses handed to them! There was no "Back Sir!" or "Get down Sir!" All I heard was the sound of wooden batons on fleshy thighs and buttocks of anyone not smart enough to return to wherever they ran from to join the fray! It was truly epic! We made our way into the station and processed our offender, as his Folks were rounded up to join him at the 2nd district lock up.

There was always something going on and it was the odd and slow times that peppered the pauses of shots fired and bullet riddled bodies. I never saw combat as a Marine. I never thought I would become a cop, especially in a place as dangerous as this one could be. In no time at all, I was helping to pull the dead out of tubs, from the side of the bed, as well as peeling them off the floor. I never got use to seeing and touching someone in a putrid state, but I will never forget what death smells like. The scent gets into everything and holds on. You can pull off your clothes and shower, and still catch a residue whiff of something ghastly that affixed itself to your nose hairs.

One-night, different partner, Officer Layton and I received a call to check on the well-being. We knew that this call meant that we were going to get a "stinker." We arrived on the scene and went to an apartment in the row houses over in Ida B. Wells. The door was not secure and slightly ajar. We knocked and the door slid open. The smell greeted us before we crossed the threshold. We called dispatch and requested the proper notifications. The Area Dicks would soon be there. Not to be gross, but the reason I hate smelling another's farts is because you don't just smell it, you can taste it! Taking in the aroma of a rotting corpse is almost like eating it. There's no holding your breath to escape it!

While in the academy, a homicide detective told us that our olfactory glands turn off after a while if confronted with strong pungent odors. He said it's best to just allow yourself to breathe it in, so that your nose cuts it off. The salves and other things can't kill it. Tough it out, or stay back. The victim was a big man, 6' 4", closer to 300 lbs. and lying in a pool of his own blood and urine. His body lay across the floor in the kitchen, near the counter. He appeared to be cooking a meal before his demise. No one else was there. My partner, being the tougher of us two stepped closer into the muck to look for identification. The thick gassy air and the sight of the body was finally getting to me, I needed to step out. Layton stayed inside and continued to look around. As I exited, the Dicks arrived. I let them know my partner was still inside. They coughed and choked on the smell. Their cigarettes and cigars were no match for the stench.

As I waited outside, the victim's brother arrived. I had to stop him from entering the apartment and I could not tell him anything about what we had found. He cried as he said, "Momma sent me to check on him because he never misses Thanksgiving! What am I gonna tell her?" I didn't have an answer.

EVOLUTION

Growing up in public housing on the southwest side of the city exposed me to a world far beyond the ordinary experiences of a child. It was commonplace to see my teenage cousins indulging in marijuana or as it was commonly known, "bud." My own initiation into this world came early—I smoked my first joint in the sixth grade at the home of my best friend.

His older siblings dabbled in selling weed and occasionally a bit of cocaine from their house or on the move. In the '70s, everyone knew where to find the local "dope house." People would drive up, knock, conduct their business, and be on their way. After my introduction to "the smoke," I started helping my friend Robert sell "Nickel Bags." For five dollars, customers could purchase a bag of weed containing seven fat, pre-rolled joints.

In those days, weed, the "low end" of the dope game, was devoid of stalks or seeds. If a seed in their joint popped and burned their upholstery upon lighting up, the buyer would find you, and kick your ass! In the '70s, the dope man was seen as a savior, offering an escape from the grind and oppression of daily life. People turned to their neighborhood "Superfly" for chemical solace from their troubles. Bud was as common as cigarettes for most—only the prudes and unenlightened shied away from the pleasure of the smoke.

Heroin remained terrifying, but cocaine was a status symbol. Our predecessors were naïve. Cigarettes were legal but deadly, and as addictive as coke. Weed, once a staple, was now a mere shadow—crushed into powder, mixed with fillers, sometimes laced with PCP, to create an unrefined cigarette-like product.

Gone were the days of discreet dope houses. Every neighborhood had them. The new wave of hustlers, emerging in the '90s, didn't sit waiting for knocks at the door or for the doorbell to ring. These dealers were out in the open, on every corner of the city's impoverished neighborhoods.

The new dope man was a child, a juvenile. Outside at all hours, he stood on street corners, bus stops, and in dark public housing breezeways, waiting for customers to stroll or drive by. Forever vigilant, and on the watch for police, rival gangs, or competitors. Armed, hungry, and desperate for cash, he ruled his patch of the city streets with gall and when necessary, steel. Younger and more agile than their adult predecessors, these new dealers evaded jail time because of their age. However, their juvenile records patiently waited for them to turn 18 yrs. old, ready to embrace them fully and drag them into the hell they had unwittingly built.

Upon the CHAPD's arrival, drug sales were conducted in plain sight. CPD's uniformed officers often seemed uninterested, ignoring transactions occurring as commonly as the sno-cone vendor pushing his cart or the hot dog vendor in New York City. The drug culture had even seeped into popular music, with the "super bad nigga" becoming a popular archetype.

When the CHAPD hit the streets of public housing, the thugs didn't know what to do about it, but made many assumptions. Like most of the viewers of local news they thought CHAPD was another security force hired to guard the property. The officers who worked contract security for housing were not the bravest bunch. The gangs were paying a few to look the other way, or to secure doors, then take their time to respond if the police were chasing an offender into the secured buildings. It was not unusual to see them do it and our command forbid us from snatching them up with the gang members when they were obviously observed obstructing our investigation, apprehension, and arrest. In plain view, the dealers boldly sold their drugs and fired their weapons into the air at will. CPD avoided coming into the buildings or driving up the fire lanes for fear of being fired upon, but this was not the way for the young blood of our fledgling department. The first class made a lot of easy arrests.

The local criminals started to strategize. "If I set up shop across the street, I'll be off housings property and they can't touch me." CHAPD officers arrested them and took them into the station for processing. After being processed, they realized that they were being arrested, and that the CHAPD was just like CPD. The dope boys were forced to evolve. They started to only sell drugs while under the breezeways, standing close to the stairwells for a quick escape. But we were young, fearless, and vigorous!

That first class of CHAPD were crafty! They were strategist! What they possessed in brains was matched by braun and guts! There was a first class officer name Winston that struck fear in the hearts of local tough guys and also in my FTO.

The thought of someone being able to break a wooden baton

on someone with one stroke is unfathomable. Once during an exchange with my FTO on proper sight alignment for shooting targets, Richmond said, "You draw down on the offender, get him in your sights, then smoothly squeeze the trigger. Boon! Boon! Boon!" he muttered over his toothpick. Winston stepped beside Richmond and said, "You mean CRACKA! CRACKA! CRACKA!" to which we all laughed.

I already deduced that my trainer, the man responsible for teaching me how to be a cop was a bigot and a racist. It wasn't that he didn't converse with us in a friendly manner, or engage in idle chit-chat. None of the senior officers did that. What tipped me off was how he casually told me and the other two Black officers I was trained with how we should engage during a man with a gun call. "Look guys, if we respond to a call, or stumble upon some mook and he has a gun, it's not stop police, or drop it, or any of that nonsense! You shoot him! If he's holding a gun, you'd better shoot, or I will shoot you! I'm not dying in the ghetto for no one!" he said as he shook a couple of spent shell casings. "But if it's a dog, don't be afraid, I'm really good with them. Let me handle it." he said, as he chucked the shell casings out of the window of the gallery. "So, shoot Black people with guns, but not dogs, because he's good with them. Check." I though. I told my fellow trainees, "I didn't take this job to become an assassin. Do what you want, but I'm not just going to shoot someone like that. I might pop a dog if it's mouth is frothy though."

Richmond's history of violence revolved around stories from senior officers about how he was reported to have shot his three kills. The first subject was on a porch, shooting randomly into the air through a hole in the metal grates. Residents reported that they heard the shooter say, "Mike, I dropped the gun!" before he was shot dead by Richmond. The second incident was while responding to a man with a gun call, where the subject was riding a bicycle. He was randomly shooting when my FTO pulled up, exited the he vehicle and shot him without announcing his office, or giving the subject verbal direction to drop the weapon. The final shooting occurred on New Years eve. Where aggressively pursuing offenders set us aside from CPD's lackadaisical attitude about when or where they chose to be "the Real Police," incidents like these shootings made even our toughest criminals cautious about what to expect from their run ins with us.

Foot chases resulted in them being caught in possession too many times, so they changed their strategies again. The dealers started dividing the tasks and risks between multiple people. One would have the dope; one would be on security with the gun and a third or fourth would serve as a lookout and decoy. This was a smarter tactic, but they could not outsmart the genius of the first class! Soon, the dope boys were stashing the "work" in potato chip bags, soda bottles, cracks in the wall, anywhere that might be overlooked during a chase.

Since the department did not have vehicles for the officers initially, the authority paid for a few rental cars to put up mobile patrols. The first class of officers were big and physically imposing. After seeing such large officers emerge from their K style rental cars, reminiscent of the popular and futuristic Sci-Fi character. This is where the nickname "Robos" came from. The rambunctious first class would load up and "slick a building!"

The look out would spot our police car coming and call out, "Robos on the lane! Robos on the lane!" then the dope boys would all scatter, fleeing to their own apartments or a safe spot! The officers would leave quickly if they did not catch anyone. Dope boys would think the coast was clear and come back out to set up shop again. Since no one was counting during the rush of blue shirts "slicking" the building, two to three officers, purposely left behind, would hide on an upper floor. Communicating with the officers in the car, waiting quietly and patiently for their queue to swoop down the stairwells to catch the fleeing subjects flushed by the mobile cop's return! Got' em! Guns, dope, money, everything! The ground officers would know exactly who to detain and where the money, dope and guns were stashed.

With nowhere to run and hide, the dope boys became more violent towards the police and each other. Rival gangs use to allow each other time "on deck" to sell and make money, but with the CHAPD in arrest mode, the Robos on the lane, they were forced to fight each other for the right to sell out of any building or development. The introduction of us into this no man's land forced change on the dope game and cause a new evolution.

FEAR

We were all growing more confident in our ability to navigate our areas of patrol and our radio ears were sharp. Richmond quizzed us constantly and corrected us every time we failed to remember an address, last location of other beats, or anytime we gave the wrong code for a call. It was a hot summer day, and we were considering taking an early lunch before we received a call of a man with a gun, located at the swimming pool off Federal just north of 4848 S. State, which housed Public Housing South. Richmond and I had just exchanged keys, so he hopped into the driver seat, and I got into the front passenger seat, with my fellow trainees in the two rear ones.

Zooming southward from our proposed lunch location off 47 street, we arrived quickly. Mike, without reducing speed, nimbly climbed and cleared the curb, slightly swerving as our tires did their best on the slick grass! Windows down, we could hear the commotion and see the activity of some people scrambling away from the full fenced in pool area. As we came around the southwest corner of the fence, I saw our gunman, weapon in hand! However, he was only a child. He was pointing something at those within the fenced area of the pool, then he sprinted away upon seeing us. The chase was on!

Richmond floored the accelerator! "You'd better get him! You'd better get his ass!" Richmond shouted at me! Time appeared to be slowing down as we quickly gained ground. His legs could not outpace our Chevy Caprice, but he was giving it his all!

Richmond, still screaming at me and repeating himself, "I'm gonna pull up on him! I'm gonna pull right alongside him and you better not miss!" As the car swerved to a stop, I exited the vehicle and reached for my weapon. The boy spun around to face me with gun in hand. This was the first time I had tunnel vision. Everything around the boy was a blur, but I noticed something was wrong. Now that I had a handgun that I carried on my hip every day, I knew what real metal looked like. The shiny gun in his hand was plastic! It was a toy gun!

I held my weapon on him and could see that he was screaming and crying. "Drop it! Put it down!" I said as he quickly released the weapon from his hand. "What were you doing with this? Why are you at the pool with a toy gun?" I demanded as I stepped closer and holstered my .357. "I was scared homey! I was scared!" was all that he could get out. I knelt down to talk to him as other units responded, and Richmond gave it a slowdown. Our man with a gun was an eight-year-old who was playing with a toy in a threatening manner. At the station, while processing him and awaiting his mother's arrival, I was glad that I did not let panic control me. As I exited the vehicle, in a real situation with a real gun and an offender that was willing to pull the trigger, he had me at point blank range. The milliseconds it took for me to correctly assess the situation probably saved his life and my sanity. While my fellow trainees and other officers pat me on the back, Richmond saddled up to me and said, "Good thing you weren't still driving, because I would have shot him."

IN THE WRONG PLACE

The narrator of the movie "Faces of Death" astutely observed that whenever a person steps outside their familiar environment, they put their life at risk. The film delved into the gruesome consequences faced by those who lived lives seeking thrills, and taking risks solely for personal pleasure. The expressions of impending doom etched on the faces of the dead were hauntingly evident. Yet, many insist they have only truly felt alive when teetering on the edge.

This theme often occupied my thoughts, contemplating the

sheer horror of the emotions and thoughts that might race through a person's mind when they find themselves in the wrong place at the right time.

In my inaugural year on patrol, I encountered numerous faces of death. More unsettling than the final expressions frozen on the victims' faces was the glee and mirth expressed by the bystanders, perpetrators, and even fellow police officers. Dispatch signaled a call for service.

"2842?"

"Go for 42."

"Take the battery in progress at 4953 S. Federal. CPD is in route as well."

"10-4 squad. 4953 S. Federal."

Upon arrival, a plainclothes CPD tactical unit and patrol car were already on the scene. Around the body of a teenaged male, there stood at least 30 to 40 young Black men, ranging from twelve to early twenties.

The youth lay amidst a mound of dirt, patches of grass scattered around the dusty bed where his battered body rested. His body twisted to the right, his head turned left and tilted slightly upward. His arms seemed as if they were in a protective stance, and his left leg was pinned beneath him. Dusty footprints tattooed his faded jeans and once-white t-shirt. Bruises marked his face, blood trickled from his ear canal, and a bloodied brick lay inches from his swollen forehead—a brutal end met through a merciless beating.

He bore no signs of gang affiliation, no "colors" to signify any allegiance. From his attire, he appeared to be the bookish "schoolboy" type, a stark contrast to the violence he endured.

Mike learned from CPD that the youth was a stranger to the area. No one present at the crime scene knew his identity or was willing to share any information. A wave of sickness washed over me, drawn to the look of resignation etched on his face.

I scanned the crowd, hoping for a glimpse of recognition or remorse from the bystanders. Instead, I was met with gloating. Just as I began to resign to this being an unsolvable mystery, answers came with the screams of a boisterous female.

"Who did it? Which one of you muthafuckas did this?" She screamed.

"Yall always fuckin' wit somebody with y'all funky asses! He didn't do nothin' to nobody!"

A moment later, another young woman broke through the crowd, her anguish palpable upon seeing the battered body. intervened to restrain her, preventing her from contaminating the scene as we awaited the arrival of the Area 1 Detectives.

"Why!" she screamed, tears streaming down her face.

"I hate y'all! All of y'all!

"What do you mean, 'y'all'? You better watch who you're accusing! Talking about 'y'all'! Better get outta here with that bullshit!" A previously silent onlooker chimed in.

The deceased was a school friend of the second woman whom CPD struggled to contain. He had just left her apartment and was on his way home when fate intervened.

Richmond confirmed CPD was handling the report, then radioed dispatch to code the call and indicate our readiness for further assignments. In that moment, I was still captivated by the lost look in the corpse's eyes. An overwhelming surge of anger brewed within me—an anger that, for a fleeting instant, wished to unleash retribution upon the crowd. I knew there were innocents among them, and despite no one appointing me judge, jury, or executioner, the injustice of this senseless violence begged for justice.

LEGENDARY

Meanwhile, on the Westside of the city, my classmate and fellow Marine, Officer Speed, was etching his name into the criminal underbelly of the Henry Horner and ABLA Homes, Ogden Courts, and the notorious Rockwell Gardens. Young and handsome, both swooning welfare queens, and menacing thugs alike, became familiar with his gold-toothed smile.

His grandfather, a reputable and hard-nosed officer of the old CPD, embodied the days when police didn't bother with warning shots, the ACLU, or your civil rights. The "old" police simply kicked or killed your dumb ass. My friend was raised on his grandfather's tales of exploits, stories of the old guard, and he carried himself accordingly.

Standing at a fit 6'4" and a lean 200 lbs., he moved like a track star, leaping fences with the grace of a gazelle, and commanded his patrol environment like a lion. Single-handedly, he took on all challengers. No one was deemed too dangerous to confront, no one was above the law. If you stumbled into the scope of his discretion, you'd better have your shit together.

While on patrol on the Southside, I often heard tales of his latest feats. Though I often worried about him, I couldn't help but marvel at his burgeoning legend. Dope boys were unaccustomed to the average Chicago Police Officer possessing the stamina to keep pace in a foot chase. But the CHAPD was a different breed. Unwilling to be caught with rocks, weed, or heroin on their person, they'd toss their "work" aside, hoping the pursuing officer would face the choice between continuing the chase or retrieval, selecting the one favorable to their escape.

Foot patrol, a daily ritual for our department members, acquainted us with our surroundings and its denizens. The more time spent outside our vehicles, the better equipped we were to police effectively. A rare "young buck" thought he could outrun Speed. He sprinted like a jackrabbit, hurling his 100-pack of rock cocaine into some bushes as he dashed madly for freedom.

It seemed to work. Glancing behind himself, it appeared he'd shaken the officer off his trail. Taking the long way home, he circled back to his building and ascended the dark, dirty stairwell to his apartment on an upper floor. The young thug entered his apartment and locked the door behind him. To his shock, waiting patiently in the shadows of the dimly lit room was Speed, calmly seated on the couch.

After taking the juvenile into custody, Speed escorted the youth downstairs to the police station for processing. It wasn't long before the boy's irate parent burst into the station.

"Who in the hell arrested my son!" she demanded angrily. "Where is that mutha-fucka? I want to file a complaint! My son ain't into this drug and gang shit! Who got him?"

"I arrested him," Speed reportedly replied softly, turning slowly to face the previously irate parent.

"I didn't know it was you, Speed." she replied, her tone now softening. "Can I see him?" she asked respectfully.

"Yeah, he's back there. Go ahead in and have a seat. It's a good thing you changed your tone because you were about to join him in custody." he said with a flash of his gold-toothed smile.

Another incident unfolded while he patrolled the Henry Horner Homes on the Westside of Chicago. Speed approached a group of Insane Vicelords gathered on a bench and along the playground fence. This gang had held sway over the neighborhood and much of the Westside since the early 70s. None of them moved, flinched, or blinked as Speed approached them. In his usual dry tone of voice, he asked,

"So, who's running this show?"

Silence.

"Y'all don't know who's in charge?"

Finally, a hard, crusty-looking brother stepped out from the crowd and came within arm's reach of Officer Speed.

"You got something to say, big fella? You know who's running this?"

"I am!" the thug asserted.

"Wrong!" replied Speed, delivering a swift pimp slap that dropped the felon to his knees.

"I run this place! From now on, this is mine, all mine!"

Gunfire suddenly erupted from an upper apartment, sending everyone scrambling for cover. Speed swiftly called in shots fired at the address and then returned relentlessly to affect the arrests, showing the knuckleheads he was there to stay.

Another tale I heard involved a concerned citizen who decided to pull over in his car to critique the young officer on his arrest technique.

"Hey! HEY! Hey, officer, you don't have to do that!" the man yelled as he exited his running vehicle, approaching Speed who was in the process of handcuffing his previously fleeing offender.

"You need to get back in your car!" Speed retorted.

"What? Who do you think you are talking to? You don't have to treat people like that!"

Ignoring the man, Speed lifted the offender to his feet and escorted him across the field to his squad car, heading back to the station to process him. However, the concerned citizen had also returned to his vehicle and was in hot pursuit. Shortly after Speed had brought his arrestee into the lockup area, the Good Samaritan stormed into the CPD District station.

"I want to file a complaint! I want to file a brutality complaint against that—" but he couldn't finish his statement. Speed had grabbed him, slammed him across the desk, and handcuffed him.

"Now you can go in for Obstruction!" Speed informed him.

After Joe Public had calmed down, Speed explained the charge.

"You're getting an Obstruction charge because you interrupted my arrest twice and followed me into a district station acting unruly. I could have given you Disorderly too, but this will do. You don't know what that man did before you pulled up, and it's dangerous to come between the police and an offender.

Now, you'll get to see the arrest process up close."

HUNTER'S MOON

A s usual, the night reverberated with the sounds of gunfire, and Richmond seemed eager for us to hit the streets.

"Rod, Dave, one of you, grab the radios. Let's move," he barked.

After a swift vehicle check, we were on our way.

"Beat 2811 is active, squad," Mike reported.

"10-4, 11 is active," came the response from Dispatch.

Riding around, Mike quizzed us on street names,

developments, addresses, and districts. He stressed the importance of not getting lazy or relying solely on using a blanket codes like "19 P as in Paul" for every situation.

Even though "19 Paul" was a catch-all code, my heart raced in anticipation, waiting for the night to take its expected turn into chaos.

Our shift started at 10 pm, but time seemed to crawl. It was past midnight, and we hadn't encountered any action yet.

"2811 squad," Mike called in.

"Go ahead 11," Dispatch responded.

"Requesting a personal at 32nd and Wabash."

"10-4. Personal at 32nd and Wabash."

"You guys can take a break," Mike said. "We might be sitting tight for a while."

While Richmond stayed in the car, the rest of us dashed in to relieve ourselves and grab some free soda. It was hard to turn down freebies, even if it was just complimentary drinks. Store owners saw these gestures as a means to build rapport, and to show their appreciation. CPD, however, would go into local establishments, restaurants, and stores, and tell the owner and workers that we weren't "real police," hoping to discourage them from giving us any discounts or freebies. Their pettiness and envy surprised me, but we weren't supposed to accept gratuities from anyone. Not us, or CPD.

Officers were allowed two "personals" per shift, a 15-minute break free from Dispatch calls for personal matters. Those 15 minutes passed in a blur as we chatted and debated how much free stuff we could snag.

"2811 is back in action, squad," Richmond radioed.

That was his cue for us to wrap up and return to the vehicle. We dashed out of the shop and back to our waiting FTO.

"Don't make me key up next time to get you moving. Good radio ears though!" Mike said as we headed towards the Dearborn Homes.

The Dearborn's, clusters of five and nine-story buildings along the State Street corridor from 27th to 31st street, were notorious. 29th street, with its small ball field, marked the border between two warring gangs in the public housing area. Like predators, our car prowled the State Street properties, then cruised the fire lane with its headlights off, of course. The alert went out among the gangsters and dealers, "Robo's on the lane!" they called. Mike scanned for signs of illegal activity and the lookout posts.

After his assessment, he rolled off the fire lane, turned on the headlights, and sped south on State Street. It wasn't a call we were rushing to; Mike just wanted to give the impression of leaving while we remained vigilant. He wasn't finished with the Dearborn Homes.

Doubling back, Mike parked the car off-road on Wentworth Avenue, one block west of Federal, between the railroad tracks and the expressway. As we exited the vehicle, Mike locked everything up, leading us up onto the tracks and down the other side, over a small fence separating us from the baseball diamond. This field on 29th street was the battleground between the Mickey Cobras and the Black Disciples.

Mike motioned for silence as he settled on the bench to the right of home plate. We sat in silence, Dave, Denise, and I exchanging puzzled glances. As the unofficial spokesman, I started asking questions.

"So," I began, "why are we out here in the open at this ungodly hour? What are we waiting for?"

Without turning to look over at me, Mike replied in a hushed tone, "First off, we're in the open, but we're invisible because the trees cast shadows under the bright lights. Secondly, between 1:30 and 3:30, it's like the witching hour down here for shootings."

"We're going to get some guns tonight, guys. We're going to see some action. Why do you always ask so many damn questions? You're like a bunch of little kids sometimes."

Almost on cue, at approximately 1:35 am, a yellow flatbed truck pulled up on the fire lane, two figures in black leaping out as the truck sped away. They brandished weapons—a shotgun concealed under a coat and two semi-automatic handguns.

"Gangster mutha-fucka!!!" they shouted, firing at the windows of an apartment on the third floor.

"KA-plow, KA-plow! Packa, packa, packa, packa!" The sounds of gunfire filled the night as we sprinted towards them, and the sound of shattering windowpanes.

Dave and I cut across the field to intercept the truck, while Mike and Denise pursued the shooters. I watched the men vanish into the lobby of a building as our partners followed in pursuit.

The flatbed never returned, and soon we heard more shots, Mike confirming reports of gunfire in the area.

"Yeah, squad, we're in the thick of it."

We searched the building top to bottom as more units arrived, but the shooters had vanished. Finally, Mike gave the call a code and we returned to 2901, where 2822 was already handling the aftermath.

"I'm sorry, sister. I can't keep coming over here," said the leaseholder sibling.

It seemed the target's family was having a card game when the shooters struck. About fifteen family members, adults, and children, filed out of the building into their cars, shaken.

"When are you all gonna put a stop this foolishness? Look at my damn windows," the leaseholder lamented.

"Repair services will be out to board up your windows shortly, ma'am," I assured her.

"This just don't make no damn sense," she muttered, walking back to her apartment.

She seemed unaware of the lucky escape, she and her loved ones who were present survived, from the hail of bullets, and the spray of broken glass. Her focus was on the shattered windows, unable to accept that it was her son who had brought violence to her doorstep. All she wanted was her windows back.

GUNFIGHT AT THE DEARBORN HOMES

For the first two to three weeks of PPO training, I felt nervous every time I put on my uniform. It was a heightened version of the anxiety I felt when faced with public speaking. However, slowly but surely, the rapid beat of my heart and the persistent dryness of my mouth lessened with each completed shift.

I started to learn the ropes of my new profession and accepted the inherent dangers that came with it.

Richmond made it a point to stick to our assigned beat.

Occasionally, he'd point out a squad car that should have been on 21st Street or cruising 54th Street, encroaching on our territory.

"Now if squad were to give those guys a hot call, they'd have to go lights and sirens all the way there because they're out of place." he explained.

Instead of circling the buildings, and cruising the fire lane, Mike parked on State Street.

"Don't forget to lock up," he reminded us, as we all stepped out of the vehicle, staying a pace or two behind him.

"See all those guys over there on the porch? Time to get your hands dirty, guys. We're going over there, and you're going to go through them." Mike directed as we approached the motionless group.

Surprisingly, no one ran. They just stared at us in disbelief. Richmond stopped a few paces before the bottom step, with

Dave, Denise, and me circling from behind him to approach the group of youths.

"Alright, let me see your hands. Everybody, hands in the air and against the wall," Denise instructed.

Dave, as silent as ever, carefully patted down each person, starting from the left, while Denise worked from the center.

I stood back a pace or two, acting as the guard officer between Richmond, and the others. I watched closely for any sudden movements from the detainees. Dave gave each one a smack on the rear as a signal for them to move along.

Denise did the same, though many of the young men seemed to maneuver so she'd be the one checking their pockets.

"Hey officer, I don't think you checked me thoroughly enough," one of them remarked.

"I did. I just didn't find anything down there. Absolutely nothing!" Denise replied.

"Oooh, she said your stash is short! Haa-haaaa!" They teased each other, their laughter and banter about to come to an abrupt halt.

Then, a teenage Black male, about 5'6" to 5'8", dressed head to toe in black, called out to the crowd we were dispersing.

"You don't wanna go to war with us! You don't wanna go to war with us!" he shouted, walking in a semi-circle, gesturing wildly. "Y'all don't wanna go to war with us!"

We were all caught off guard. I saw Richmond clenching his toothpick between pursed lips, his teeth grinding. Mike started walking toward the youth.

The teenager quickly turned and sprinted back down the fire lane toward the MC buildings. We followed Mike's lead, with Dave and Denise leaving the rest of the group to investigate further.

I wondered what had prompted the boy to call out like that. Did he see the police and think we'd protect him, or was it a warning to the GDs, a promise of impending violence?

As I stepped into full view of the ball field and fire lane, automatic gunfire erupted!

"Budddddd-buddddddd!" followed by a sound I'd never heard before, "Whimm-whimm-whimm-whimm!" The whine of a bullet nearing its target. The youth's warning seemed to foretell the latter.

Who was under attack, the GDs or us? I wasn't sure, but we all sought cover along the side of 2901 Dearborn.

"2811, 10-1 squad, shots fired at the police! 10-1, 10-1!" Mike yelled into his radio.

The shots grew louder as bullets whizzed by, hitting the ground and the dumpster beside us. Dave took position along the southeast wall, Denise beside him in the corner, Mike behind a tree, and me kneeling beside him and the dumpster. The footsteps of our assailants echoed off the project walls now. We all had our weapons drawn. Richmond held his in his right hand and his radio in his left. In the moments between the first shots and Mike's call to dispatch, they closed in on us.

"Rod, take my radio!" Richmond said, turning to me.

Why was he telling me to take his radio? I wondered.

"Rod! Take my radio!"

Could he not see my hands were full? Why was he insisting I take his radio?

"Rod!! Goddammit!!" Mike's voice rose as he threw his radio to the ground, stepping out from behind the tree into the line of fire. He discharged his Smith and Wesson .45 caliber semi-automatic at the approaching attackers.

It was as if a divine hand struck down the one closest to Mike. The shooter fell to the ground untouched by the Hydro-Shock casings Mike was known to carry.

The offender's weapon slid a few feet, coming to a stop near Mike's feet. The other shooter vanished into the lobby, possibly escaping to a safe house without any blue shirts to pursue him. Richmond stood over the downed shooter; weapon trained on him. The acrid smell of gunpowder enveloped us as the silence settled in the aftermath of our brief gun battle. Dave, Denise, and I stepped from the shadows onto the fire lane with Mike.

"Let us have him! Give that motherfucker to us, Robo!" the BDs demanded, moving closer.

Mike turned toward them; weapon drawn. "Stay back, or I'll shoot where you stand!"

Taking advantage of the distraction, the shooter rolled over and scrambled to his feet. He ran like a rabbit, weaving and crouching across State Street toward the EL tracks and the cover of darkness.

Mike quickly turned his weapon and gazed at the fleeing felon, only to watch him disappear. I wanted to chase him. My reflex was to pursue, but I didn't dare step into Mike's line of fire.

The other units began to arrive on the scene. We policed the brass or spent casings. I pocketed one as a souvenir. Mike gave it a code and requested a slowdown from dispatch. Every one of the PPO's working that night wanted to know what it felt like. They all wanted to know how it felt to be involved in a shooting. After my shift was over and I made it home, Jason came by and disturbed my sleep.

I had a good story to tell him this time, and showed him my shell casings. He still had a few weeks in the academy to complete, but he seemed to have regrets about not staying with us.

While he marveled at last night's tale, I couldn't shake the thought that I could have been killed or maimed in a three-minute gunfight at the Dearborn Homes.

RICHMOND GETS BEAT DOWN

"2811, take a ride to 3547 S. Federal, apartment 607, on a Domestic. A neighbor called to report a male juvenile fighting with his mother and grandmother."

"10-4, squad."

It was a routine call for service, presenting an excellent training opportunity for me and my fellow PPOs.

"Dave, Denise, you'll join me on this call. Rod, you stay with the vehicle," Richmond directed.

Stateway Gardens was notorious for car vandalism, and leaving our vehicle unattended could lead to days off or, at the very least, severe reprimands from the watch commander. By leaving me behind, Richmond ensured the safety of the car until our return.

Instead of parking near the entrance, Richmond pulled into a space on the Federal side of the building.

"Why are we parked all the way back here?" I inquired.

"You mean a whole 30-35 feet? Maybe, it'll be harder for some asshole to chuck a can of creamed corn at the damn vehicle, fuck if I know? Come on, you guys. For fuck's sake!" Richmond responded with sarcasm.

As I settled into the driver's seat, I watched them disappear briskly into the dimly lit building corridor. Counting the windows up to the sixth floor, I noticed a gathering crowd on the gallery. Within five minutes, I saw a blue shirt slam against the metal grating of the porch.

My fingers flipped the radio's microphone volume up, but there were no transmissions from Dave or Denise. The crowd's cheers, oohs, and laughter filled the air as Richmond struggled amidst a mass of bodies, his white arms flailing against dark figures. His hat fell, as he stumbled repeatedly against the fence.

"2811! 3547 S. Federal, 10-1 squad, 10-1!" I yelled into the mic, closing the windows, locking the doors, and hastily exiting the vehicle.

"Dammit!" I cursed as I realized, "The keys, I didn't grab the keys!" Glancing at the still running vehicle, then up at the gallery and Richmond's blue shirt, I dashed into the darkness towards the stairs, and the commotion.

With the speed of a track star, I raced up the greasy, gritty steps in the stairwell until the echoing voices surrounded me.

At least fifty people crowded the area, blocking my path to the scuffle. Drawing my baton, I entered the porch without breaking stride.

"Get back! Back up, back the fuck up!" I commanded with fierce authority.

Instantly, the crowd complied, parting to reveal our suspect pummeling Mike mercilessly, while the other PPOs stood motionless. I waded into the center, landing blows on the six-foot man-child's thighs, buttocks, right side, left side, shouting orders.

"Get down! Stop, police! Get down, now! Do it now!"

He attempted to swing at me, but my baton struck faster, landing sharply on his arm, the sound of flesh meeting wood echoing through the chaos. Richmond scrambled to his feet, grabbing the assailant from behind as I continued to strike. Together, we wrestled him against the fence.

The crowd's laughter turned into muffled comments, and sporadic outbursts as Dave and Denise remained among them, watching.

Quickly, Mike cuffed the suspect, and we led him towards the stairwell and out of the building. Additional units were arriving as Mike radioed dispatch for a slowdown. Then came the moment I dreaded.

"I made a mistake and locked the keys in the car when I was coming to help you." I confessed.

Mike stood there; teeth clenched on a fresh toothpick. Stepping in, he radioed for another unit to bring extra keys to our location.

"Squad, can you have a unit run an extra set of keys to my vehicle at this location?" he requested.

"10-4, 11."

Soon, the keys arrived, and the squadrol volunteered to transport the prisoner. Richmond, meanwhile, relayed our situation to dispatch.

"Put 2811 in route to the Taylor Station with one for Aggravated Battery and Battery to a Police Officer!" he announced.

"10-4," came the reply from dispatch.

The ride back to the station was silent. When we entered through the backdoor, Mike faced a barrage of questions from senior POs who hadn't been present.

"Hold on a sec, fuck. Dave, you do the complaint; Denise, the arrest report; Rod, the case report. I'll be back to check them." Richmond assigned.

Exiting the room, he engaged in a conversation with others, making sure his voice carried enough for us to hear. Amidst his colorful recounting of the incident, there was one shining moment.

"This fucker was wailing on me! Faster and stronger than I thought. I was trying not to hit his mom and grandma when they tried to intervene, but damn, he kept nailing me! Then I heard a voice cry, 'Move, get the fuck back!' I thought it was one of you guys. It was my PPO! Fucking Dukes come busting in, and Dave and Denise didn't lift a fucking finger! Them fuckers!" Richmond exclaimed.

Suppressing a smile, I couldn't help but relish the unexpected praise amidst the reprimand aimed at my partners. Later, Mike thanked me for taking the initiative, but questioned whether Dave and Denise were suited for this line of work.

BEING THERE

After completing my probationary period, Dave became my first regular partner. We stuck to the old routine of stopping by 32nd and Wabash for a drink and a snack, then cruising around the fire lanes until we got a call for service. Sometimes we'd try to knock out our building checks early in the shift. Building checks were handy for knowing where the vacant units were, to spot criminal activity, such as stash spots for weapons or dope. Quite often, the gangs would use them to shoot from the windows. While it wasn't uncommon for some officers to take shortcuts, sometimes by submitting older reports, we chose to conduct a full one each shift. We usually found something through our diligent searches.

Dispatch called us, "2831!"

"Go for 31," we replied.

"Check the well-being, possible domestic in progress. 4848 S. State, apartment 1009."

"10-4 squad. 4848, 1009, domestic. In route."

We pulled up on the lane, jogging briskly up the stairs on this cool winter's eve. As we approached our floor, a young male came around the corner, then brushed past us. Dave grabbed his arm, "What's the rush, my man?" he asked.

"I got somewhere I need to be!" the guy replied.

"Must be really important, the way you pushed past us." I said.

"Nah, my fault. I just became a father. I gotta get to my girl.

She's waiting on me downstairs," he explained.

"Don't let us hold you. Congratulations!" I said as I watched him go.

As we entered the apartment, we knocked, but the door was partially ajar. Flashlights in hand, we made our way towards the rear of the apartment, checking each room to ensure it was clear before moving on. In the rear bedroom, there was a young woman, late teens, heavy set, wearing a nightgown, but not much else, sitting in the window with one foot on the floor and the other out of the window.

I hate the cold. Being anemic, no matter how warmly I dress, the cold always manages to cut through the material and through me. This apartment was freezing, and she was barely clothed.

"Ma'am, we received a call of a disturbance. Are you okay?" I asked.

"I'm good. It's over now. It's done, I'm tired. I can't take this no more." she said, as she stared out into the dark, starry night.

"Well, ma'am, you're hanging out of a window. There must be something going on." I stated.

That's when she told us that her boyfriend had just left the apartment. Days earlier, she delivered a preemie, their child, but he also had another woman pregnant and in delivery at the same time. He decided he wanted to be with the other woman and their new baby, leaving her and this child alone. She also shared with us the story of how her mother committed suicide, and that she felt like doing the same. She said she was tired of everything and didn't want to hurt anymore. I knew then that the guy we encountered on the stairway was the fleeing father.

"So, help me to understand something. Your ex did all this to you, and instead of throwing him out of the window, you decided you'd jump? Is that correct?" I questioned, injecting some humorous sarcasm.

At that point, she shifted her weight on the windowsill as she turned towards me. Her eyes grew wide, and the chubby cheeks of her smooth, deep chocolate skin rose, revealing a beautiful, albeit teary-eyed smile.

"You cute!" she said, immediately becoming flustered and slightly embarrassed.

"Thank you," I replied, smiling back.

"Oh my God, I'm up here, hair all over my head, looking a mess!" she exclaimed, totally distracted from her initial plans but still one leg away from a 10-story drop.

Unknown to me, CFD (Chicago Fire Department) was on the scene, standing to the rear of us. I asked her how old she was when her mother died. Then I pleaded with her to consider that loss and its effect on her. I cautioned her to consider what her new baby might endure if she chose to do as her mother did. She stepped back into the apartment, and my partner closed the window.

"Do you have a girlfriend?" she asked sheepishly.

"Oh yes, we're engaged." I replied.

She smirked and said, "The good ones always are."

I offered her information and a phone number for counseling, urging her to speak with a professional. As we exited the apartment, I realized that I might have saved a life, two lives. This was one of those instances that served as a reminder that policing isn't always about aggression or the chase. Sometimes you just have to be there for people.

NEW YEAR'S EVE 92'

New Year's Eve was an unusually dangerous night in public housing. I had heard stories of cops hunting punks, and thugs stalking the police on this night. Because of the tradition of citizens marking the occasion by stepping out onto their porches, and hanging outside of their windows to shoot in the air at midnight, it was the perfect opportunity to disguise shots fired in vengeance.

Of the many tales I heard, during the previous New Year's Eve, was a frightening one about my FTO. While we were still in the academy, he was involved in a shooting. As I recall the rumor, he and his partner responded to shots fired at an address in the Robert Taylor Homes. As they entered the breezeway of the building, shots rang out from a darkened stairwell. Mike returned fire, and the volley stopped. Cautiously, he and his partner rushed to the stairwell where the shots rang out from, but the shooter was gone.

After searching the stairwell and walking every gallery in the building, they gave dispatch a code and left the area. Later, at the end of the shift, Mike was called in for a roundtable with CPD because a man showed up in a local ER with his bullets in him. He had related his injuries to the same location where officers responded to the shots fired. Later, when he told the story to me and my fellow PPOs, Richmond said that he was taken to view the body, but couldn't confirm that this was the man he shot at, because of the darkness of the porch, and in the stairwell. So many no-no's, but like we were told in the academy, things on the street occur differently from training.

BOOTY ON DUTY

Whenever a group of adults gather, someone is bound to have feelings for someone else. Office romances are nothing new, but among police officers, they can be risky, if not downright amusing. I wasn't lucky in love on the job. No, I didn't get any action on duty. I wasn't bold enough to pursue it while on the clock, but I was certainly hoping to catch the attention of one of the department's attractive women.

Back in the academy, all the guys (and probably a girl or two) lusted after classmates, as well as a few of the instructors. Out of respect, I won't name this one, but she was the epitome of professionalism, with an easy-going personality to match her very feminine physique. Her caramel-colored skin and high cheekbones framed her captivating smile. She was simply gorgeous. The instructors were on their best behavior with us recruits, but there was a drama or two that was too sensational to keep hidden from office gossips.

My military training taught me to keep a subordinate's place, but my classmates seized every opportunity to weave sexual innuendo into our discussions.

There was another female instructor, who was married to a cop, but failed to see the indiscretion of sleeping with her spouse's best friend, who was also an officer on CPD. Her husband and his friend exchanged gunfire, over their love triangle, outside of a district station. One ended up in the morgue, the other in jail. Meanwhile, the hot-to-trot instructor found solace in the arms of another academy mate. No matter how dangerous or risky a situation might be, some people seem attracted to risky behavior.

I tried to make a move on a coworker or two, but the funniest situation in regards to my feeble attempts, involved a woman who became a good friend. Officer Sara Henry was her name before she married. She was dating a coworker of mine, but rumor had it that they'd split up. She didn't work in my station, but I ran into her one morning after hearing the gossip.

"Uh, hey Henry, what's up?" I said, startled to see her.

"Hey, what's up?" she replied dryly.

"You got a minute?" I asked, smiling.

"Yeah, what's up?" she said, as we stepped off to the side by the vending machines, impatiently peering at me with a furrowed brow.

"I was just wondering, is it true that you and Kane broke up?"

WHAM! She hit me full force in the chest with her clenched fist.

"Stay the hell out of my business!" she yelled as she stormed away.

"Ow!" was all I could manage to say, as I rubbed the spot of impact. I didn't quite understand where my conversation went wrong, but as she rightly said, I was poking my nose where it didn't belong. I walked out of the station, nursing the pain in my chest.

The most embarrassing incident I can recall involved two CPD patrolmen and an open mic. Due to the equipment cops carry on their duty belts and the snug fit of car seats, it's not uncommon for an officer to lean on their key, and inadvertently broadcast their conversations over the microphone.

The unnamed couple was working a beat car out of Public

Housing South, near our Robert Taylor Station. While trying to coax his female companion into giving him some oral action, if she did not want to go all the way, either he or she were broadcasting the conversation for all to hear. Dispatch repeatedly warned units to watch their keys, in hopes of allerting the two that their conversation was no longer private.

"Come on now. Come on and do this for me." he urged.

"Alright then, I'll take care of you baby." she replied.

The rustling of the seat interior could be heard as the following conversation was broadcast.

"Oooh baby, you look like you're ready for me."
"Come on girl, come get it!" he eagerly responded.

The sound of clothes rustling, and a zipper opening followed.

"Aww, look at him. He's just a little fella!" she giggled, followed by faint slurping sounds.

Of course, everyone in the district recognized their voices, and the male officer was teased with that classic line, whenever his coworkers needed a laugh.

After working with female partners for a while, my perspective shifted. Most of the women on the job were as assertive and efficient as any of my male partners. However, I did find myself taking a more protective stance when working with them, in comparison to my male counterparts.

I realized it was my fault for not seeing or treating them as equals. I could blame being raised in a misogynistic culture for this failing, but the truth is, I was still very immature at the age of 26. It was for the best that I never established a real relationship with anyone during my career. How could anyone remain completely professional in a violent situation, involving a lover or someone I had grown to desire? I had to let go of thoughts of romance on the clock. No more thoughts of booty on duty.

DON JOHNSON

on Johnson, the actor, was the epitome of manliness, with his rugged good looks and portrayal of one of the coolest cops on television in "Miami Vice." The show provided a glimpse into the drug culture of Florida's underbelly. Tonight, however, I found myself on patrol with the Suburban Chicago version of Don to my reluctant Tubbs. This Don was unassuming, standing at about 5'9" to 5'10" tall, weighing around 170 lbs., sporting coke bottle lens glasses, bad skin, and bad breath that smelled like he ate the tabacco he preferred to chew and spit all night, while rocking a mustache akin to Magnum PI.

For some reason, I seemed to be getting all the rejects of the watch assigned to me. As a PPO, I rode with whoever the watch commander designated. Seasoned cops were often paired up, akin to a marriage or a "work spouse." These two-person teams were usually inseparable, sharing the same days off, and making formidable arrests when working together. Putting misfits in a car together, however, only resulted in a long and troubled night.

I had seen Don in roll call and around the station, but we'd never really had a conversation. Since I was always one for small talk, I decided to strike up a conversation during the vehicle check to get a sense of his approach to policing.

"So, ready to roll, man?" I asked.

"Yep, got everything I need from my locker," he replied, clutching his metal binder.

This was one of the first times I'd seen an officer carry

that aluminum box that doubled as a container and writing surface. It seemed too bulky for my taste and likely to clutter the already small space we had in the front seat of the cage car.

We took a quick ride to 32nd and Wabash to grab some beverages and began our shift. "2831," Dispatch called out. "Go for 31 squad. Check out loud music at apartment 1504, 4950 S. State."

"Will do, squad," I responded. We took a swift ride up State St. and cut over to take the fire lane. It was standard procedure to take a direct approach and pull up in plain view when answering a call. It alerted everyone to our presence, and hopefully, the offending neighbor would take the hint and correct the issue before we arrived. Either way, we still had to investigate.

Don kept driving. "Where are we going?" I asked.

"They put it in the C.O. Book not to park on the lane. I'm going around back," he explained.

I twisted my face a bit, thinking, "Great." I thought to myself, as I fought the urge to be a front seat driver. I sat quietly and let him approach the building his way but warned him not to park too close to the building, because residents might throw things from the windows. As we walked into the breezeway, we made our way to the elevator, which Don preferred over the stairs. I sighed.

Once on the floor, we walked the porch and knocked on the door of apartment 1504, but no one answered. Since there wasn't any music coming from the apartment, we called it in to Dispatch. "19 Paul squad, and we're clear," I radioed.

"Why didn't you just give it a 4 B-Boy? It was a disturbance with music," Don questioned.

"Because I didn't feel like it," I responded curtly.

"Well, don't you think it's lazy to use a 19 Paul when there's a specific code for it?" he pressed.

"How about you mind your own business?" I shot back, feeling my irritation rise.

His face reddened a bit as he stood there, staring at me. "Ooooh, he's mad. Good," I thought, hoping he'd just shut up. We walked out of the building in silence. A few steps onto the sidewalk, a can of corn came whizzing down from above, crashing near our feet.

We quickly moved away from the sidewalk, scanning above for any more incoming objects.

"Ha-haaaa, muthafuckaaaaas!" a voice shouted, followed by laughter from above.

We stood there for a moment, watching for a head to peek out from the apartment we'd just visited. I was ready to head back, but Don wasn't having it.

"Let's roll," I said.

"Nah, let's just leave. We won't be able to get in, and we already called it in," Don suggested.

"Hell no! You can't be throwing canned corn at the police and get away with it. We were lucky not to get hit," I retorted, growing angrier.

"I'm not going. I'll be in the car," Don said as he headed back.

I stood there alone for a moment, then followed him back to the car. "Fuck it," I thought, frustrated by the turn of events.

"Donny, my man, I think it's time to hit the streets. Wanna go bust some dope boys?" I asked.

"Sure, whatever. Which building do you want to hit?" he replied.

I had him drive us around State and Federal to scope out the area.

"Let's go for 5101," I decided.

They were doing construction at 5101 S. Federal, with a huge mound of dirt obscuring part of the building. I directed Don to park on Wentworth Street.

We approached the building under cover of darkness, creeping into the stairwell on the hidden edge. I led the way through the shadows and across the grassy areas to avoid getting our shoes caked in mud.

Once inside, I gave Don some quick instructions.

"Turn your radio down or off. Put your keys somewhere they won't jingle. Try to step lightly on the edge of each stair as we jog up to the third floor. Keep your hands off the banisters just in case someone's watching from above. We'll run up, head down the southern stairwell, and then it's game on!" I explained.

I shot him a smile before taking off. I loved this part—stalking these boys, the chase. My heart raced, and my breath quickened with each step.

In the dusky stairwell, the cool air brushed against my arms, but beneath me, behind me, there was a faint sound.

"Errnnt, errnnt."

I made it to the third floor and waited for Don to catch up, but that sound persisted.

"Errnnt, errnnt."

I looked back at Don, and as he approached, the sound grew louder. I held out my hand, signaling for him to stop where he was. I walked closer to him, motioning for him to come closer to me.

"Errnnt, err-nnt,…err-nnt."

"Dammit!"

It was his shoes! His goddamn shoes were squeaking. I lost it.

"Fuck it, let's go!" I said, no longer bothering to keep my voice down.

"What?" he asked as I stormed out of the building and back to the car.

He hurried after me, asking what he had done wrong, but I was done with it. I resigned myself to a long, boring night devoid of any arrests, thanks to Mr. Noisy Shoes.

HUNTER/PREY

In the 70s, Mutual of Omaha sponsored a nature-based television show called "Wild Kingdom." One of its most vivid scenes to be etched into my memory is that of a cheetah chasing a Gazelle. The graceful dance between hunter and prey, the fluidity of the chase—it's a remarkable sight.

The Gazelle sprinted, zigzagging to alter its course as the cheetah relentlessly closed in with every stride. Finally, the cheetah leaped, effortlessly bringing down the Gazelle. The clash of the leopard's claws against the muscles of the ill-fated gazelle, followed by the powerful snap of razor-sharp fangs into adrenalin filled sinew vanished, lost in momentary resistance and the growing cloud of dust. It's a primal, savage moment as the hunter claims and immediately feasts on its prize.

For me, the thrill of the chase was always the highlight of policing. I aimed to rid my patrol areas of their criminal elements, but I didn't want it to be easy. I didn't care if they surrendered quietly; secretly, I wanted them to run. I silently dared them to.

The younger they were, the more likely they were to challenge you. To a teenager, a person in their twenties or thirties seemed ancient. They believed they could outrun you, outwit you. Isn't it the folly of youth to feel invincible, or to think of oneself as immortal? The young never seem to grasp that their elders once felt the same, only to later confront their mortality. It was the chase that rejuvenated me, bringing back my youth, my vitality, and my power!

Every time I arrived on a scene, I studied the body language of those I approached. Watching for sudden movements, scanning for cues that hinted that my subject had thoughts of flight. Another sign of a potential runner was observing when their face is turned towards you, but their body is subtly shifted away towards an exit. For those subjects, I'd move slowly towards the direction they telegraphed with their body, but I was hungrily waiting. Once their body and head aligned, in a direction pointed away from where I was standing, the race was on.

I was always quick on my feet. As a child I loved to run and as a teen, I was often able to catch city buses before they could reach the next stop. Thanks to my Marine Corps and police academy training, it was my increased fitness and endurance that set me apart from most of my peers.

One night, while on foot patrol, exiting northbound from 4950

S. State Street, we entered the playground nestled between 4950, 4948, and 4947 S. Federal. There, a lone teen dressed in black stood, slowly backing away as we approached.

It wasn't a crime for him to be in the playground at eight in the morning, but his nondescript attire and sudden movement away from us raised suspicion. Drug dealers and shooters often donned basic black from head to toe—it was their uniform. I smiled as he picked up his pace, walking backward.

"Good morning! Heading somewhere?" I called out, grinning.

He chuckled, returning my smile, then turned slightly towards the adjacent building's gallery. We were about a quarter into the playground, approximately 100 feet apart, and he had trotted towards the far edge, about 20 feet from the building's entrance. I would have to double that distance to close the gap if I wanted to catch him. I called out once more.

"Hey, don't make me chase you!" I shouted, chuckling, but he didn't heed the warning. I liked that.

With a swift turn, he bolted as I pulled out my wooden baton, drawing in a deep breath. The chase was on.

Our initial steps were synchronized, but I watched his feet, lengthening my stride to intercept him. He wasn't as fast as he thought, for I made it through the playground before he was within ten feet of the breezeway. The burn in my thighs was palpable as I pushed against the unyielding pavement. He could hear me closing in.

My prey tried to outwit me as he entered the building. Stomping his feet, zigzagging to fake a decision towards the stairs, aiming to lead the chase upward. I mirrored his movements, matching his stomps to let him know I was gaining ground, and almost upon him.

"You know I've got you, right?" My voice echoed as we dashed through the building and towards the next.

"Ahhh! Ahhhhh!" he gasped.

"Come here!" I growled, leaping onto his back as he attempted a last-minute change of direction.

"Ahhhhhh! Momma!" He screamed as we hit the moist grass, me still riding his back, clutching his coat collar.

"Boop," came the sound as I lightly tapped the back of his head with my baton.

"I told you not to run, didn't I?"

I cuffed him, rolling him over. During the pat-down, I discovered a 50-pack of rock cocaine on his person. This was a significant bust, one that would hold us over easily until lunchtime.

DENNIS AND MALCOLM

Growing up in a strict household, then going off to the Marines, made me a stickler for the rules. As a police officer, I always wore the proper uniform as it was intended. My uniform was clean, creased, and my shoes were polished or patent leather. I wore my hat, or cover as we called it in the Marines, at all times. I embodied the role I portrayed, and I expected the same from those around me. I had been conditioned to respect authority, and to follow the chain of command.

Well, that attitude of mine was put to the test by the new class of officers. While the first class consisted of serious-minded, seasoned police and correctional officers, aged 30 and up, my class was a band of 20-year-olds from all walks of life who were molded in the image of our senior trainers, and the sum of disciplines taught in the Chicago Police Academy. The third class, in my opinion, was a rowdy bag of rebels, roughnecks, knuckleheads, and legacy kids of Chicago Police Officers who had done something which prevented their acceptance onto CPD. Also, the first lateral transfers from various suburban departments arrived, and with them standards and expectations contrary to our current workplace.

We also welcomed our first large batch of White Officers, some of whom saw policing in public housing as an opportunity to flex their authority, and as they put it, "kick some Black ass!"

That small, but bold bigoted few quickly found out that if they messed with the right ones, their play time would be short-lived. There were a couple of new White officers who were rumored to be beating up on subjects, and then locking them up, whether they had probable cause to arrest them or not.

The gang members watched a particular team, stalked, and ambushed them. They beat those officers asses so badly that they were hospitalized. Believe it or not, criminals treat honest cops with respect, or they use to. If you were professional and "fair" to them, there were no hard feelings. If you caught them in a foot chase fair and square, no harm, no foul. If there was a pursuit, and they were able to ditch the fruits of the crime, but you were the type of cop who held on to a stash of dope, or a gun to "put a case on them," they cried like babies! It was not fair. It didn't matter to the offender that they were dealing dope every day, dirty as dirty could be. It was the fact that you did not catch them doing their dirt. You were cheating! You "put something on them that they did not have."

It is also a criminal offense, for the cop, which is another reason it shouldn't happen. Criminals expected you, as the law enforcement officer, to play fair. As the "good guys" you above all else should follow the rules. Our department was starting to receive new officers that were rumored not to be playing "fair."

While my class worked feverishly to prove ourselves to the senior officers and fit into the department's culture, this new bunch didn't care one bit about acceptance. They were just as young as we were, but they had their own ideas about how to spend their time on patrols.

However, there were two newbies who stood in stark contrast. They also seemed to greet me with distaste anytime we occupied the same space. They were Officers Dennis and Malcolm.

It was probably my fault. My face often betrays my true feelings. I am sure that they could see my disapproval. Who was I to judge them anyway? Still, I hated how they wore their earrings and necklaces exposed while in uniform.

It looked unprofessional to me. Both officers seemed to come to work looking dusty, and purposefully disheveled in their appearance. I could hear my Drill Instructor's voice screaming, and ringing in my ears, "UNSAT! UNSAT!" meaning, unsatisfactory!

I remember giving Malcolm some shit about the Pooka shell choker, he proudly displayed through his unbuttoned, long-sleeve shirt. Those cuffs rolled-up, of course.

"It's hot out. A short-sleeved shirt could have solved your wardrobe problems this afternoon." I quipped.

Dennis chimed in with a scowl, "Mind your own damn business DUKES!"

Then Malcolm, ever the smart ass, retorted, "Hmmf, not sure why you're wearing sneakers. It's not like you do anything around here, besides riding the oak. Desk Bitch!"

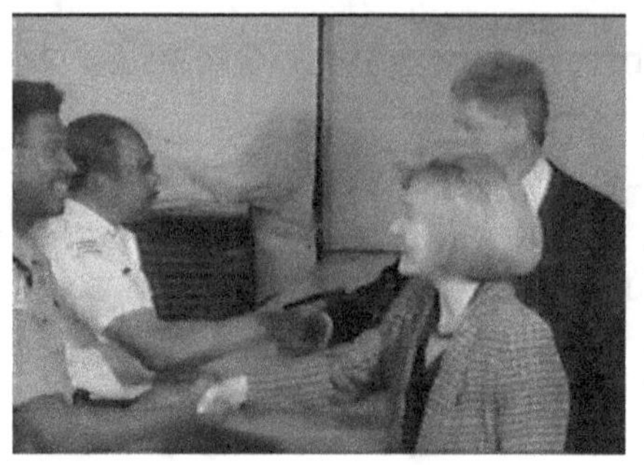

Did this little fucker just call me a bitch? I thought, feeling my face tighten. Malcolm and Dennis leaned into each other and their squad car, reveling in the burn that Malcolm delivered. My jaw clenched a little tighter. I wanted to fire back, but I found myself empty-handed and without a good come back. "Y'all don't know me! You don't know how I get down! Ask anybody!" I responded, as I tried to save face.

They just laughed harder. "Gone, man. Gone in there to the desk where you belong! Don't nobody want to hear about what you used to do!" Dennis taunted as they climbed into their vehicle to leave the station.

Their appearance on the clock aside, those two were hell on

them boys in the street! They were good cops, in every way, the real police! Instead of abusing their authority, or robbing dope dealers of their cash, they were the kind of officers you'd want on your side, ready to roll up and take action against anyone doing wrong on their watch. No job was too big or too small for them to handle. I didn't know it then, but over time I grew to respect and idolize them. They just always looked like they had rolled out of bed.

One night, while working a hire back shift with Rick, a senior officer, we were having a pretty uneventful evening. Both of us had chosen to pick up 8 hours on our day off. Hire back was paid double time and a half, for officers to serve in a security function, at certain trouble spots. If there was a call for service at the location we were stationed at, and an arrest was made, a unit would come to relieve us, or handle the paperwork.

Rick and I didn't do a damn thing that night. However, when it was time to be relieved of duty, our ride and replacement had not arrived. To my unpleasant surprise, Dennis and Malcolm were there to take us back to the station. They rolled up, we hopped in.

"So, what took you guys so long to pick us up?" I asked.

Malcolm fired back. "You know what? Your asses could have walked. You could use some exercise!"

I decided it was best to just sit back and be quiet until we got back to the station. I didn't want to argue with his sawed-off ass. I was anxious to change clothes and go home.

As Malcolm was pulling into a parking space at the station, Dispatch keyed up with a call. "Units, we have a large disturbance, men with guns, in the vicinity of Ida B. Wells!"

Rick and I had opened our doors to exit the vehicle, but Malcolm slammed the transmission into reverse, stepping on the gas! We both flipped forward, the passenger doors opening wide, then abruptly slammed shut when he hit the brakes, swerving the rear end of the squad car around to point the car's nose towards the exit, and onto the street.

"Man, what the fuck you doing?" I demanded.

"Y'all didn't get out fast enough! We gotta get this call! We'll drop y'all off after!" Malcolm shouted back, hyped as hell. I was pissed!

"10-4 squad! Put us in route!" Dennis said, looking over at Malcolm and chuckling.

"I don't see a damn thing funny!" I said, showing my disapproval. But as we got to Wells, the threat grew closer and clearer.

"There you go! That's something funny right there!" Malcom said, in response to the crowd of one hundred plus men and boys in the street and lining the sidewalk! As the mob saw us coming, lights and sirens blaring, it paused.

Malcolm sharply cut the wheels towards the fire lane, jumping the curb as we swerved towards the crowd. The car came to another abrupt stop, and Dennis and Malcolm quickly exited the vehicle, batons in hand, while screaming, "Yeah, motherfuckas! Aaaaaaaaaaaaaaaaaah!" as they charged the crowd!

Like a herd of cattle, the mob ran through the dust cloud kicked up by the vehicle. Some were tripping and falling over each other, but all were trying not to get caught! Me and Rick looked at one another, laughed, and joined in the mayhem. Soon, other vehicles were arriving, but most of the boys and men had run home or into safe havens in the surrounding buildings. There were a few arrests, but it was crazy how the night ended in such a crazy way, thanks to those wild ones, Dennis and Malcolm.

CHAPTER 5 – FALLEN – AS TOLD FROM THE POINT OF VIEW OF OFFICER SARA HENRY

I t was a Thursday. I was assigned the 3:00 to 11:30 shift. We were all signing up to work as much overtime as possible. It wasn't often we'd get the chance to earn extra money, and special assignments paid at time and a half. Vince Lane, our chairman, received a call from one of the residents, alerting him to an attack on the CHA Maintenance crew working at her building and the destruction of the wall.

The local drug dealers saw the CHA buildings and surrounding property as theirs. How dare the housing authority decide to build a wall to enclose the first-floor gallery? How dare they do anything without the thugs' consent? The punks were in a rage. They attacked and ran the construction crew away, then used the deserted tools, their hands, and their feet to topple the wall at 4525 S. Federal.

The original construction of the buildings left the first-floor gallery open. The upper floors were fenced in to prevent the residents or their guests from breaking a limb or falling to their deaths. It was Lane's plan to build brick walls to enclose the lower galleries as a means of limiting access to the buildings. He also decided to place security officers inside every lobby to check the identification of the residents and to monitor the flow and location of their visitors.

Less than a third of the buildings located on the Southside were already enclosed and had a team of two to three security officers posted 24 hours a day. However, the clusters of buildings at this location were some of the biggest money-makers for the Black Disciple street gang that controlled them. The dealers needed the space wide open to allow their customer base ease of access and to give themselves room to flee at the slightest alert to police presence.

Upon inspection of the crime scene, Mr. Lane held his anger until he reached the Robert Taylor Station. Lane wanted to confront the watch commander and discover for himself how a band of punks could get away with assault, battery, and destruction of CHA property. The sergeant was in the station, but he was caught off guard by the chairman's arrival.

"Hello, sergeant. How many units do you have on the street?

How many late cars or plain clothes units? I need to know because the workers at 4525 were attacked, and the wall they were building was knocked down. I need to know how this happened on your watch. I need to know why you are watching television instead of patrolling the district and monitoring your troops!" Lane questioned.

Dissatisfied by the answers he received, Lanc demoted the sergeant to patrolman and decreed that there would be a car placed on that building on every watch and every day until he said otherwise.

Vince Lane fought long and hard to get the residents the protection they needed and deserved. He instituted programs that improved the residents' standards of living, and he refused to bow or back down from any confrontation with our criminal element. Unknown to him, our thugs were already receiving pressure from another source.

BD's Vs. GD's

The Black Disciples were a homegrown public housing offshoot of the city-wide lords of violence, the Gangster Disciples. The gangbanging drug dealers that lived in public housing had it made.

Each of the buildings in Robert Taylor was sixteen stories tall, contained ten apartments per floor, and housed at least one adult per unit. Add to this the multitude of relatives and visitors to the various public housing locations, and the dealers had a warehouse of customers to sell to.

The bulk of the Robert Taylor Homes was bordered by Federal Street to the west and State Street to the east. Buyers would exit the expressway, go under the railroad tracks two blocks east to Federal, or boldly pull into various parking lots along State Street to make their drug purchases and roll back onto the major thoroughfares, to quickly leave this squalid area to enjoy their high.

The Black Disciples were part of the Gangster Disciple family. The sentiment of most families is that family sticks together, supports one another, and shares their wealth. The BDs were getting very wealthy, and their brothers in the GD Nation promised that they would not lose any sleep if they had to go Cain and Abel on them.

First, the BD's tried to coax their public housing rivals, the Mickey Cobras, MC's, to assist them in keeping their brethren out of their territory and pockets. The MC's decided that being allowed a few hours out of an evening to sell in buildings the BD's controlled was not enough incentive for them to join in this family feud. Maybe it was best to allow this family to collapse upon itself and reap the spoils.

When I came on shift, I didn't have a partner, so I was placed in a car with Jimmy Haynes and Derrick Powers. Both had served honorably in the Army during the Vietnam era. Powers and I were newbies from the second class of CHA Police, but Jimmy was one of the original PO's that pioneered this department. Jimmy was easy-going, but all business when it came to policing and patrolling public housing.

During our tour of the building, not much happened. It was a normal shift, even quiet if you don't count the occasional sounds of gunfire in the distance or random explosions of half sticks of dynamite. We rousted the thugs from the lobby area; partially to disrupt any business they might have been trying to generate but also to seek cover for ourselves.

We couldn't park the squad car on Federal because the GDs would open fire on the building, cars, and residents from the railroad tracks from time to time. We had to park the vehicle in the front of the building, far enough away not to block the fire lane but close enough to keep an eye on and access when our shift was done. The first-floor gallery was the only safe place to stand.

Other than the occasional complaints about not being able to stand around in the lobby from the BD's, it was a regular shift. Unknown to us, our relief had been waiting on the side of the building. Now that Officers Pucceh and Layton were on post, we were free to leave.

We were walking across the fire lane to get into our vehicle and return to the station. There was approximately fifty feet between us and home, then all hell broke loose. There was a barrage of gunfire. I'm not sure what direction it was coming from, probably from 4500 S. State Street, but we began to run for the vehicle as fast as we could. Powers was the first one to reach the vehicle and immediately sought cover. I was almost there, and then I heard someone say, "Help me." I looked back, and it was Jimmy. He had been hit.

SILAS HELPED

Time stood still. I couldn't move; it felt like an eternity as I stood there in the hail of gunfire, watching him call to me. My legs wouldn't budge. I was so focused on him that everything else in my line of sight blurred and disappeared into the silence. Then came the sound of voices cheering, a roar akin to what you'd hear at a sporting event. "Ha-haaa! Hell yeah, we finally got one!" I heard them cry.

Someone appeared, breaking me from my stupor. A resident dashed from the building into the rain of bullets, pulling

Jimmy out of the line of fire. Suddenly, I could move. We both grabbed an arm and hurriedly pulled Jimmy to the vehicle. Powers drove us to the hospital, while I sat in the back with Jimmy.

I tried to keep Jimmy calm, diverting his thoughts from the pain. "You're going to be all right, Jimmy. Just think about your family. Think about your wife and kids," I said. Powers reached around and tapped me, shaking his head no, silently indicating that things might not have been good at home for Jimmy at that time. I didn't know him well, or anything about his personal life. I was just trying to keep his spirits up.

We arrived at Mercy Hospital. I jumped out of the vehicle, rushing frantically into the ED. Finding an orderly, I informed him that my partner had been shot, then hurried back to the vehicle. The medical staff quickly came to our assistance, cautioning us not to move Jimmy. They were concerned we might worsen his injuries if he wasn't handled properly.

The team swiftly extracted Jimmy from the car and secured him to the gurney, wheeling him away. That was the last time I saw Jimmy alive. I stood in the waiting area, time passing strangely, hours feeling like mere minutes. Word of the shooting spread rapidly throughout the city and the housing authority.

Vince Lane's response to the crisis was swift. He granted overtime to every available employee to secure and inspect the crime scene. From police officers to security staff, administrative personnel to general laborers, everyone was on site to assist in the effort.

The Superintendent of the CPD, though a vicious critic of our fledgling department, lent as many patrolmen from his organization as he could spare to block street access and assist with transporting our prisoners. There were few times, past or present, when our departments would mesh so well and work together as we should, but we were one family that day. We were all blue.

After his shift, Victor Hamilton stopped by.

"Sup, Sara? You alright?" he asked.

"I'm straight," I said.

We stood together in silence for a moment before I had to go. I returned to the Taylor Station. It was Friday, payday, and it didn't make sense to go all the way home just to turn around and come back. Besides, I had a wedding to attend the next day, so I wouldn't be coming in anyway.

I'd been planning all week to call in sick on Saturday. I couldn't have predicted the night we had, but one thing was certain— I wouldn't be showing up for work. I didn't finish until 9 am. I sat in the locker room, waiting for my check.

Saturday morning, I spoke to Sgt. Evans and called off on medical grounds. He was hesitant at first to grant the time off. He was concerned that if I didn't come back in, I might not come back at all, like falling off a bike or a horse. But I was okay, I thought. I took the time off and returned the following Monday.

Jimmy Lamarr Haynes died on August 17, 1991. He wasn't the last officer to be wounded in the line of duty, but he was the last to lose his life.

ROBERT BROOKS

It was 3rd Watch the day after the Haynes Shooting. Dave and I listened to the concerns voiced by the watch commander. We were all cautioned not to take unnecessary risks during patrol and to be vigilant upon entering and exiting locations. I didn't know the details behind Jimmy's shooting, but I had no intention of becoming the next victim.

Within 24 hours, our department, with assistance from every agency within housing and CPD 2nd District, shut down all unauthorized traffic and illegal activity from 47th to 43rd and State St. CHA Security now manned buildings previously under contract security firms. Overtime was offered to any patrolman or staff willing to help root out non-residents from the buildings along the State and Federal corridor.

Right after roll call, Dave and I were given our assignment.

"2831, take the Criminal Trespass to State Supported Land at 4548 S. State St. See security for details."

"10-4, Squad."

Some serious security haters existed among our ranks, but I aimed to rise above the pettiness. However, the overzealous ones, while well-meaning, often got in our way. The worst served as lookouts for the dealers and thugs.

Some argued, what choice did they have but to cooperate with the criminal element? They were posted at the same locations daily, easy targets for anyone seeking revenge. My take? If they felt it was too dangerous for the salary, they should quit.

Everyone had excuses for not doing their jobs, but CHA Police were out there every day, refusing to be scared off.

Dave and I arrived at the address and parked behind the building. Security was eagerly waiting.

"We thought you'd never come! We were about to handle it ourselves!" one exclaimed.

"Come on now, that's not necessary. What happened?" I asked.

"That guy hit me! He's going to jail! I'm signing complaints!" the irate security officer said.

While Dave spoke with the calmer security officer, I asked the agitated one to start from the beginning.

"This guy walked in, tried to get on the elevator. I asked for I.D. He pulls out a Jailhouse I.D.! I said, 'No, you need a building I.D.!' I asked if he lived here, and he said yeah, in 608! So, we checked, and his name wasn't on the lease. I told him he couldn't go up unless the leaseholder signed him in as a visitor. That's when he snapped! 'I just got outta jail, I'm tired and wanna lay down!' he said. I told him to wait until someone signed him in, then he punched me in the jaw and ran up the stairs! He stole on me, man! I was trying to help him! I want to press charges!" he recounted.

I glanced at Dave, who was clearly trying to suppress a smile. I took the I.D. from him to see the offender's face, Robert Brooks.

"Keep an eye on the side stairwells. Dave, take the elevator; I'll take the center stairs," I directed.

Arriving at the sixth floor, I waited for Dave. When the elevator opened, I entered the door to the gallery for 608.

There stood a shirtless, muscular Black man, approximately six feet tall, and at least 200 pounds. We often assumed males with extreme upper body development and thin legs were fresh out of jail. His relaxed stance, even as he leaned against the fence with his back to us, suggested he was stronger than both of us combined.

"Hey Rob!" I said, reaching for him. He didn't turn around.

"Are you Robert Brooks?" I asked, placing my left hand above his right elbow.

"Naw!" he replied, trying to step away.

"Don't pull away from me!" I commanded, reestablishing my grip just above his elbow. His dense flesh tightens within my fingers.

"Dave, let me see that," I said, taking another look at the I.D. before handing it back. I already knew we had our man.

"Turn around, face the wall, and place your hands behind your back. You're under arrest for Battery to a Security Officer and Criminal Trespass to State Supported Land."

"I didn't do nothing!" Brooks protested, trying to snatch his arm away.

I was ready. Squeezing the nerve in the joint of his elbow, I reached for my baton—only to realize I'd left it in the vehicle. Debating whether to break policy and use my flashlight as an impact weapon, I held on.

"Let me go! Let me at least get a shirt!" Brooks demanded, as residents gathered to watch.

"Let that brother get his shirt," my partner interjected, grabbing Brooks, and leading him towards the apartment.

Stunned for a moment, I realized I was losing control of the situation. An officer should never let an offender return to a dwelling or anywhere to retrieve anything. With adrenaline rushing, I snapped back into arrest mode.

"Aw, man, gon' let that brother get his shirt," Dave urged, but Brooks suddenly broke free and took off running.

Dave chased, but I knew I was faster. He was in my way. Brooks reached the entrance to the rear stairwell and slammed the door shut. Dave struggled to open it, and I joined in the effort.

Together, we managed to force the door open, but as Dave stumbled through, Brooks kicked him in the knee. As Dave went down, I leaped over him, feeling my flashlight pop out of its ring.

As I watched it tumble down the stairs, Brooks made his escape. I took a deep breath and sprinted up the stairs to close the gap.

Touching every other step, my thighs burned as I pushed myself faster, chasing Brooks up five or six floors. I kept count in case I needed to call for backup. He began to tire, clinging to banisters as I raced up, using my legs to skip stairs without breaking stride.

"Can you hear me? I'm comin' for you! Wanna make me chase

you? Your ass is mine!" I shouted over our pounding footsteps and rasping breaths.

As we reached the same staircase, I closed in, just a couple of paces behind. Brooks turned to run up the next flight, but I reached over the banister, grabbing the back of his pants and yanking hard. This sudden halt allowed me to grab him by the throat with my free hand as we fell backward towards the metal door.

Maintaining my grip, we crashed against the wall. Brooks's weight bore down on me, his hand reaching for my weapon. I shifted, driving his face into the wall to my left. He elbowed me, but my vest absorbed most of the impact. I released his pants, putting him in a rear naked choke hold.

He gasped, flailing as I tightened my grip, cutting off his air. But Brooks wasn't finished.

As he reached for my holster, I shifted my weight, driving him into the wall. We locked eyes, inches apart. His gaze said, "my turn," but my fear fueled my next move.

Cradling the back of his skull with both hands, I rammed my forehead into his nose. He screamed. Locking my left arm around his neck, I attacked the pressure point behind his ear with the knuckle of my right hand. Squeezing him tightly, I alternated between punching his jaw and applying pressure.

Suddenly, I heard the sound of handcuffs.

"Time to go to jail now!" I declared, grinning.

"Fuck you! I ain't goin' nowhere!" Brooks shouted, kicking as he hit the floor.

"Oh, yes you are!" I countered, trying to grab his wrist to put him in the escort position.

Brooks went limp, then kicked out as Dave intervened.

"Dukes, damn, let me get him! Just chill!" Dave urged.

"Fuck you! I said angrily, frustrated that things had spiraled out of control.

"What took your ass so long anyway?" I demanded.

"Shit, I had to limp all the way up here and I grabbed your flashlight!" Dave replied.

"Fuck a flashlight!"

"Time to go mutha-fucka! Get up!" I said, refocusing on Brooks.

Grabbing his legs, I started dragging him down the stairs. He struggled, pulling a foot free and swiftly kicking me in the chest. I fell back into an unsecured firebox, the door catching my shirt. Brooks laughed.

Ripping my shirt to free myself, Brooks attempted to make a run for it.

"No, you don't!" I exclaimed, kicking Brooks in the ass before he could clear the first step!

He tumbled down the stairs, rolling as he fell. I leaped down the flight, landing heavily on my feet as Brooks lay face-first on the landing.

"Done running? You're gonna get enough of running from me!" I said, snatching him back up to his feet as I applied a steel wristlock.

"I'm gonna sue! This is police brutality!" Brooks protested.

"Not yet!" I replied, struggling to restrain him.

A voice called out from a few floors down.

"Rob! Rob, you okay?"

"They're beating me! Call the police! Call the real police!" Brooks yelled.

We were both winded, but the battle wasn't over. Within sight of his friends and others standing on the landing, Brooks made one last desperate dash.

"Help me, somebody! Somebody, help meee!"

With the last of my strength, I wrapped my legs around his, pulling back on his arms to take him down again, wrestling on the concrete porch. I called for backup, realizing I was too tired to contain him alone.

Within minutes, every unit was on the scene.

"What you got, Dukes? You good?" they asked.

"Just get this mutha-fucker!" I replied, rising to my feet.

As the others took the elevator, I made my way down the stairs, gun in hand. Exhausted, I exited the stairwell and headed to the car. The heat and stress caught up with me, and the next thing I knew, I woke up startled, surrounded by fellow officers. I had passed the fuck out.

Back at the station, the watch commander reamed us out for needing medical attention over a misdemeanor offender. We finished the paperwork, and another car transported Brooks to the Deuce for us. After being seen at Mercy, I was glad to be back in my vehicle, on my way home.

Driving home, and for every waking second after, I replayed the arrest in my head. I realized I needed to start weight training. Had Brooks intended to fight instead of run, the outcome could have been bad for me. The next day, I bought a rack system and started lifting weights on a regular basis.

ROCKWELL

Known to me as a child as "The Rockwells," it was a development on the westside known for one thing, guys who loved fighting the police! Seriously. They craved and actively sought opportunities for fighting the police. Whether we were driving by, or coming on location to answer a call for service, we knew and expected to have to "humbug" for a minute just to get into the building. They relaxed on that with CHA officers after a while because we weren't running or ducking when it came to throwing some hands. Our female officers would scrap too! Those women would take you down, or hem you up without batting an eyelash! The Rockwell boys quickly learned that if they wanted to start something with one of our officers, be prepared to get whupped and processed.

Throughout public housings locations, we did what was called "sweeps.' Citywide and at random, a location would be determined, CPD would be notified to assist with logistics, transport, and lock ups We usually found a respectable amount of rock cocaine and weapons, unless someone on the advisory board was a friend or relative of the main gang leader or drug dealer controlling the area. It was common for mother of the leader to be in meetings as a representative of the families in the building to be in meetings with housing and police officials as the plans for the sweeps were being devised. They knew the date, time, and location in advance! Those were the days that we wouldn't find a damn thing.

Once while doing a sweep in Rockwell Gardens, one of the officers nearby had one of the city's zone radios. This is what we heard.

"10-1! 10-1!" the voice said.

Units, do we have a 10-1? Dispatch came back.

Static and keying of the microphone could be heard along with muffled sounds and scuffling!

"Aaaaah! Aaaah! 10-1 squad! 10-1!" The voice came back screaming again!

"What's your location unit?" the dispatcher came back, sounding calm but concerned.

"Aaaaaah! Aaaaaaah squad! Aaaaaaah! The voice screamed!

"Officer, tell me where you are so that we can send you some help!" dispatch responded, then started calling roll to determine which beat was unaccounted for. That would allow them to determine the unit's last location if, they were currently in their assigned sector.

It seemed to take forever to get that unit an assist. A true fist fight is usually spent within three to five minutes if you are both going all out, fists, elbows, and knees! The officer that was monitoring the zone left our assigned post, so we did not get to hear the aftermath of that exchange. One thing is for sure, if that officer was tangling with some joker in "the Rockwells," he should have known to knuckle up!"

EVERYTHING IS NOT ALWAYS AS IT SEEMS

I awoke feeling like hammered shit. I was tired, achy, and every other thing that made me want to skip work. Well, that was almost three hours ago. I feel perfectly fine now. Although I called off work as soon as I got up, I felt better and didn't want to waste 8 hours of vacation, even if was a for Saturday. I called the watch commander back to inform him I was coming to work, changed into my uniform, and made it there before noon.

It was a beautiful day—sunny, not scorching, with extraordinarily little humidity. If only "homie" could take a day off, it could be a relatively easy day. To my surprise, I learned that I would be the third man on a car with P.O.s Milton Nelson and Bruce David.

David didn't talk to me much, but I always figured he was a cool person. He appeared to be the serious and laid-back type. The only time I ever saw him laugh or smile was around Phil, his regular partner. Nelson was another story. I try to give people the benefit of the doubt, assuming they are cool with me, and not out to just fuck with me because they think they could. I prefer to get along, or at least, be cordial. Nelson didn't allow me that space. He had an aggressive personality, constantly expressing his anti-police rhetoric, while being a cop and wearing the uniform. He also belonged to the Nation of Islam. I wondered if he was confused or at odds with himself, but either way, I wasn't looking to convert him to my mindset, nor did I want to adopt his. I was just hoping the time I spent on the car with the two of them would not be a long one.

I didn't even get a chance to put my things down and get a radio before David told me we had to get going because we had a call.

"How did we get a call this fast?" I asked.

"Dispatch got it from the zone. It's a check the wellbeing," David replied.

"CPD's lazy ass gave us their call? That's some bullshit! It's probably a fuckin' stinker. Damn!" I said with disgust and anger.

"Hey man, we've been holding on waiting for you to get here. Now it's time to take this call, so let's go," Nelson chimed in.

"Man, shut the fuck up!" was what I was thinking, but I just looked at him as we filed out of the building to the squad car. At least it wasn't a cage.

We arrived at the building and took the stairs up to the apartment. It was odd that there weren't more people out in the lobby or on the floor of the gallery. Nelson took a break from his propaganda to bitch about why we all had to go to the call. David politely let him know that if he was going to the call, we all were. I was concerned with the validity of the call. The gallery windows had grating installed for security, and the residents had adopted the ghetto security of removing the doorknob.

We all stood clear of the doors and windows as David knocked with his Maglite. He knocked a couple of times, the sound echoing off the walls of the porch. I'm sure everyone on the porch, if not the building, could hear us. There was no answer. I knelt to peer into the diamond-shaped opening of the doorknob's rod and could see nothing but daylight shining from the bedroom adjacent to the apartment entrance.

I sniffed at the hole and examined the window. The guys were wondering what, or why I was doing that. I was looking for an accumulation of flies and trying to detect an odor of decaying flesh. We had all experienced finding a stinker. Thanks to CPD's crooked past, patrolmen transported bodies to the morgue to have them pronounced dead instead of an EMT or medical examiner. The body would then be taken to a funeral home that was paying the CPD officers off. This scheme forced individuals to have to pay to get their loved ones transported from that funeral home, to one of their choice. Otherwise, the body was held hostage until someone paid. Now, it's just a regular task that was written into their roles and responsibilities that most officers could do without. I didn't see or smell anything out of the ordinary.

The neighbor from apartment 04 came out to talk to us. She said she had not seen the leaseholder in almost two days.

"I talked to her Thursday. She was so excited that her man was getting out." She said.

"Coming home from jail?" We asked.

"Yeah. She was Bar-B-Q'n, and we had some drinks, you know, but they got to arguin' and the party was over," the woman said.

"Were they just arguing, or were there any punches thrown?" I asked.

"I didn't see anything, but I did hear some bangin' around through the walls yesterday," she related.

"Any idea what time you heard it?" David asked.

"Sometime yesterday afternoon, I think. Y'all are the second ones to come here. CPD was here this morning."

"Really?" We all replied.

"Yeah, the police were banging on the door about 6:45 this morning. Somebody came to the door, and then slammed it in their face!" she said and laughed.

We got a description of the couple and thanked the neighbor for her help. We huddled together on the porch and agreed upon a plan of action. I wanted to force the door or window to gain access. Nelson wanted to give it a code like CPD did, say fuck it, and leave. David contacted the watch commander and tried to figure out if there was a maintenance person or building manager who could let us into the dwelling. We were in luck. The manager was called, and we stood by for her arrival. In the meanwhile, we reflected on what we learned. Neither the leaseholder nor her companion had been seen in almost 24 hours. According to the neighbor, CPD answered the call but left without solving the issue because we answered it almost 4 hours later. Why would they just blow off the call if someone answered the door? It didn't make sense.

The manager showed up and asked why we needed entrance to the apartment. Satisfied with our answers, she looked through the set of keys to find the one we needed.

"If y'all gon' go in, I'll stand by out here with her," said Nelson.

I didn't want to mess with the dead either, but from the looks of things, I expected the apartment to be empty. The manager was willing to go into the unit with us, but David asked her to stand by while we secure the premises, then she could enter.

With the door unlocked and weapons drawn, we swiftly entered the apartment. I went into the kitchen and checked the main closet to make sure no one was hiding. Before I could say clear, I heard David call out, "We got one...shit, we got two!"

Dammit, now we are going to be stuck here all day waiting for CPD to process this mutha-fucka! I thought. As I rounded the corner to make my way towards David, he screamed, "Stop mutha-fucka, drop it!"

As I entered the hallway, descending deeper into the apartment's interior, the air grew thicker with the scent I had been searching for earlier. It was visually cloudy from the putrid gas seeping from the bloated and blackened body that seemed to have collapsed in the doorway. Seconds clicked by. I was now side by side with David and could clearly see the subject of his alarm.

"Stop! Drop the weapon!" David commanded as the offender crouched where he once lay, repeatedly stabbing and cutting at himself.

David with his arms extended, locked his eyes locked on his target.

Too much was happening too fast. Flies buzzed in a frenzy

around our heads, drawn to the decaying mess at our feet. The leaseholder's companion was a gruesome sight, blood soaking him with every brutal slash of the knife. I couldn't let David fire his gun. I had to act, but I didn't want to risk getting shot or cut.

Grabbing a five-foot-tall plant from the hallway, I lunged forward, using it as a makeshift staff to block the knife and knock the offender off balance.

"Move, get that shit out of the way!" David's voice was urgent as he holstered his weapon and pulled out his baton.

I dropped the plant, ready to assist, but David was already moving. His baton struck the man's hand and forearms, commanding him to drop the knife.

"Do it now!"

The blade clattered to the floor as we both demanded he get down, but he resisted.

David wrestled him to the ground, hands grappling with the bloody mess. I hesitated, not wanting to touch the gore, but I knew I had to. With a knee in his side and another on his shoulder, we managed to get the offender cuffed.

"2832."

"Go ahead 32..."

I relayed to dispatch: "Notify the watch commander we have one deceased and one in custody. Contact CFD; our offender has multiple self-inflicted knife wounds."

The body lay just a few feet away, surrounded by buzzing flies and the sickly-sweet stench of death. Questions swirled in my mind, but David remained composed, relaying our situation to the authorities. I just wanted out of that room.

Nelson stayed outside, setting up a perimeter as other units arrived to assist. CFD responders were on the porch, ready to take our bloodied offender for medical attention.

David was busy speaking with the watch commander and Radney, our latest Chief. I thanked the building manager and started on the paperwork. I couldn't bring myself to go back into the apartment. Trying to write against the wall, the ink in my pen refused to flow. Kneeling on the porch floor, I continued to write, feeling the weight of everyone's eyes on me.

"Are you okay?" Someone asked behind me.

"Yeah, I'm good," I replied with a forced smile.

But I wasn't. I needed a moment to process, but duty called. The Chief approached, and I scrambled to my feet. He praised our work, and at that moment, I needed to hear it. It pulled me out of whatever dark thoughts had consumed me.

As the area Dicks arrived on the scene, we had to re-enter the rooms to brief them on what we found. CPD's presence always grated on us, especially the way they seemed to undermine our department. But today, amidst the chaos, they needed information, and we needed their expertise.

Two CPD plainclothes officer seemed particularly interested in our findings, wanting to enter the crime scene. Nelson informed them they could, but only if they provided their names and star numbers for the record. They declined and quickly left.

Gusts of air from the door and bedroom windows dissipated the fog of bodily gases and flies that had accumulated. Further inspection of the apartment revealed powdered cocaine in the kitchen, a mound of weed on the coffee table, and various prescription medications in the rear bedroom.

The woman's body, twisted and darkened, partially blocked the bedroom doorway. She was unrecognizable, her identification found amidst the remains of her dead flesh.

"It doesn't look like her, she's so dark," I murmured.

The detective paused, then spoke, "Sometimes with heavy drug users, the body decays at a faster rate," before turning away to continue the examination.

Our prisoner was taken to Cook County for care, and it was our turn to take over. We stood by with the officers we were relieving as the Dicks attempted to interrogate the offender.

"Sir, we need answers to what occurred last night," one detective said.

The man, weary and defiant, replied, "You keep asking the same shit. I ain't answering no more questions. Just leave me alone, I'm tired."

I stifled a laugh, understanding the seriousness of the

situation. The forensic pathologist entered the room, signaling a break in the interrogation. David and I watched as they spoke with the detectives, leaving us with the prisoner.

"There are no signs of trauma on her body. We believe she died of natural causes," the pathologist reported.

"This is bullshit," one detective muttered as they stormed out.

I was shocked by the diagnosis. My mind raced, piecing together the events. The couple, fueled by drugs and alcohol, had argued. At some point, the woman collapsed, possibly dead, in the doorway. Her companion, in a haze of substances, either failed to realize or chose to ignore her condition. When CPD arrived, he armed himself, leading to the chaotic scene we had just left. Maybe in his stupor, when we came into the apartment, he thought it was the original officers he closed the door on. Was he distraught because of her death and sought to

end his own life, or was he afraid he was going back to jail for

being found with her body?

We had all been convinced our captive had killed his mate in

a drug-fueled rage. We were wrong. All of us. Everything isn't

always as it seems.

CHAPTER 6 - THE FUNNIES – INTRODUCING, THE WEEZEL

I never intended to create a comic series, not to mention several. They seemed to spring to life on their own. The first sketch was inspired by the looming threat of a mass exodus to CPD by the majority of the first and second class of police. This urge to vacate our department followed upper management's disregard for our requests for better equipment and the promised pay raises we had not received. We were promised a starting pay of $24K, but only received 19K. Since we were all state-certified peace officers trained under the Chicago Police program, every officer interested in leaving was professionally qualified to fill the vacancies on the city's force through lateral transfers. Two weeks back in the academy and boom, switch patches on the uniform and don the checkerboard! Done!

CHA appealed to the City of Chicago not to dismantle our department by accepting our officers. Given our existing training, the city stood to save millions by taking us in instead of spending it on processing new recruits. Chicago agreed, and only two officers slipped through the cracks to become CPD. CHA closed this escape route by cutting training time and curriculum for future classes to ensure that these officers would need retraining if the city ever reneged.

Even though I had just convinced my childhood friend to take the opportunity to stay in the academy and switch departments to become CPD, I had no desire to leave CHAPD.

I felt at home working in the projects. I felt purpose policing there. Much of my life had been spent playing and visiting the properties I patrolled. I felt necessary here.

To illustrate the anguish and tease the frustrated aspirants who were dreaming of making the cut to escape our department to CPD, I created the first "no-name" funny:

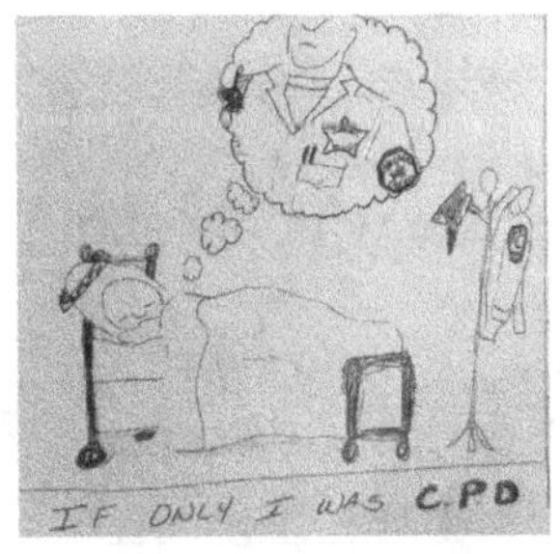

"If only I were CPD, I'd be the Real Police! I could be a fat, lazy slob, and everybody would still kiss my butt! And I'd never have to play security guard ever, ever again!"

Someone liked the comic enough to post it on the bulletin board, and I began to bask in the anonymous notoriety. Next, I created a short serial about the dread that most officers experienced at the thought of working New Year's Eve. I depicted a hard-charging officer from the first class as a "superman" and added two new aggressive and effective drug officers as our department's "dynamic duo."

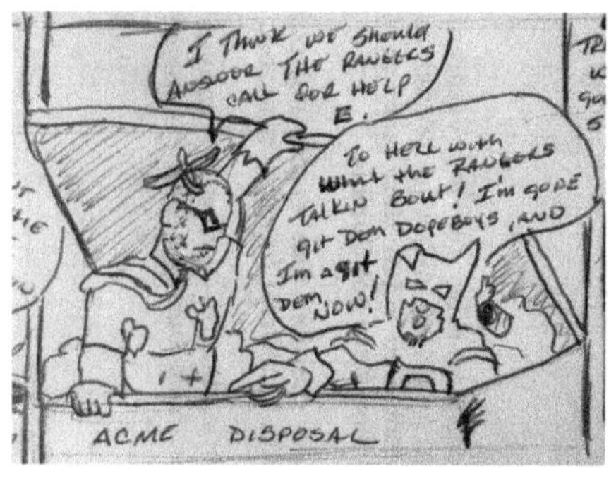

The Ranger, E-man and Upshaw were the stars of my fictional account of our most dangerous night on patrol. E-man and Upshaw were created as a generic dynamic duo. Since E-man was short, I drew him in a bat suit that was big and ill fitting. Upshaw was his robin like sidekick. I had a lot of fun with those characters and years later, after my identity was revealed, we had dueling strips that were inappropriately gross for any workplace, but my audience loved them, and the viewership grew.

The more laughs the funnies got, the more I wanted to create. For a while, they were an easy way to tease friends and ridicule enemies. However, rapid changes in our rank structure, in-house politics, shifts in our daily mission, and the myriad problems the officers faced became the focus of my comics. I began to draw them in an editorial fashion and created an avatar to speak for me and the rest of the troops. I created the Weezel!

No one knew that I was the person who created the funnies, for at least five years. It was fun being anonymous. I could eavesdrop on conversations, soak up department gossip, then convert it into funny stories that informed and entertained us. It was also very cool to hear praise and admissions of fear from officers who did their best not to "end up in the funnies."

As good as we were as a department, we still had officers who managed to mess up, act out, or do something stupid, like irritate the Weezel's handler, which was of course, me. Anything outside of professional behavior was enough for anyone to make the funnies. Other artists tried to copy The Weezel's style and duplicate my characters, but they were quickly rejected by my readers, which was just about everyone in the workplace. Another anonymous officer from the third class took a shot at parodying two sergeants, who disagreed violently about the much-needed vacation time from the job.

It became the most memorable funny that I did not create.

Not to be outdone, I took advantage of the rumor mill and used the power struggle for control of our department between the current Chief, and an ambitious sergeant. I called it "CHA Wars." As a parody of a popular sci-fi series, I mixed fact and fiction to match the real-life players to scripted characters. The series was well-received.

However, the fun and games were about to end.

Throughout our existence, CPD had been resistant to our presence, but the City of Chicago was finally able to wrest control of housing properties and employees. As officers began to polarize racially on patrol and watches, and as upper staff, sergeants, lieutenants, and commanders jockeyed for power and control of our personnel. The mayor played the first card in a hand that would eventually topple our police department. CPD's current chief and HUD Chairman took command of our department.

The rumor was that they were sent to assess what could be of value to the city and CPD, and then they would dismantle us. I created the "Toy Cops" series to chronicle those events. The first comic depicted the chairman urging the new Chief to do

as he pleased with the "toy cops" they were left to play with. What followed were regular episodes of the Weezel poking fun at our bosses, ridicule of their lack of support, and a spotlight on any foolishness on their part.

There was always a patrolman willing to supply me with material to keep the funnies current. The episodes that spoke to the hypocrisy of the standards and expectations we were held to, versus the support we were given to complete those task became more difficult as our new masters began to bind our hands tighter and tighter.

Those actions made the funnies more relevant to my readers and a daily escape for patrolmen and bosses alike. The Chief and chairman were said to have sent drivers to stations to get them a "funny" at the start of their day. They reviewed

them like the morning paper! The motor pool flipped seats in vehicles to find the latest edition of the funnies, instead of the work order for our dilapidated squad cars.

There were a couple of instances where the Chief read a cartoon and learned about something that had not been reported through proper channels.

Several years after the demise of the department, I was talking to an officer and close friend of mine who also starred in a few funnies. He told me that while he was processing the crime scene of a homicide for the suburban department he transferred to, a state trooper approached him and asked,

"Do you wanna see something funny?" and handed him an episode of the funnies called "Da Preacha's Wife."

"Do you wanna hear something funny?" Mike asked.

"I know the guy who drew this." He replied.

COMBO ... DA PREACHER'S WIFE.
DO YOU TAKE THIS WOMAN?
I BEDDA, SHE MIGHT WHP MY ASS
...AFTER YOU GET MY CHECK, PICK UP A 40, SOME HERB AND UH... A PORNO. HEH HEH JUST KIDDING.
MEANWHILE AT ALTGELD...
GOOD THING I'M SO FINE.
I DIDN'T TAKE THIS JOB TO SLAVE DAY IN AND DAY OUT. I JUST WANT TO GET PAID.
HERE GIRL. GO TO WORK
WHAT CAN I DO YOU FOR?
GOT I.D.?
I'M HERE TO PICK UP HUDSON'S CHECK.
NO.
WELL I DON'T KNOW YOU. NO I.D. NO SERVICE. HIT THE BRICKS! GIT TA STEPPIN' BABY!
AW DAMN! TELL ME TROOPERS DON'T TAKE DIS KINDA SHIT FROM NOBODY!
UH... JEFF...
IT'S OKAY. GIVE IT TO HER. THE LORD WILL BLESS US SEVEN FOLD FOR THIS.
THANK YOU SGT.
OH NO SHE DIDN'T!!!
DOINK
FLIP
THANKS FOR THE PEN... RAGGEDY ANN!!
IT'S ON NOW! GIVE YOUR SOUL TO GOD BECAUSE YOUR ASS IS ALL MINE!
GRRR.
AFTER I COME FROM 'ROUND THIS COUNTER, I'M GONNA SET IT OFF!!!
WHO SAID I WAS GONNA LET YOUR NAPPY NECK ASS GET FROM BEHIND THE DESK!
AND LIKE A PACKAGE FROM UPS JANICE'S MAIL WAS AIRBORN! WITH EACH HAYMAKER THROWN...
AW, FIRST YOU WUZ A MONSTER. NOW YOU IN SHOCK!
MS. HUDSON BEAT A LESSON INTO JEFFERS THAT SHE WILL NEVER FORGET.
IN PUBLIC HOUSING EVEN THE DESK ON PAYDAY CAN BE CONSIDERED AS HAZARDOUS DUTY.
"STANKY"!! YOU GOT KNOCKED THE FUCK OUT!!!
HEY YOU FUNKY GIRL. REMEMBER WHEN IT COMES TO GOD'S PROPERTY THE TRUTH IS THE LIGHT!

CHAPTER 7 – REVELATIONS

Juvenile Officer/Internal Inspections

After six years of regular patrol, I was actively seeking to join a special unit. Although I helped plenty of new officers through PPO training, I passed on the opportunity to become an FTO. I did not feel that I had enough experience to train new officers. The dance between my arrogance and self-consciousness continued to play with my psyche.

I also passed on the opportunity to take the sergeant's exam.

Of the bosses we had that I respected, I doubted that I could fill their shoes. The wealth of their experience and people skills was far beyond what I had attained and dealing with the pettiness of CPD was a task within itself.

I wanted to be the kind of boss that could walk into any Chicago Police District and hold my own in a professional, yet forceful manner, without embarrassing my men or the department. However, some officers just wanted higher pay and prestige of rank.

The wanton violence of regular patrol started to wear on me. The patient patrolman that stood and chatted with the roughnecks was becoming impatient and prone to snap judgments and quick decisions. I was saved by becoming one of the first and only juvenile officers for the CHAPD.

Joe P. Mayo was respected by many in Illinois law enforcement, but more so within CPD. Because of his former title as commander of CPD's Juvenile Officers, he was able to pool his connections and resources to create our first and last team. I say last because after all the training and certification we received, the project died a quick death after our current Chief ousted Mayo within days of him setting the program into motion.

Maybe Murray didn't realize how crucial Mayo was to CPD allowing us to work within their system, but we were cancelled in a heartbeat. At least I have a story or two to share about my experiences.

On the day that we were assigned to CPD's Juvenile Officers for on-the-job training, I was immediately thrust into a hot case. At approximately 8:45 am I accompanied one of my trainers to investigate a sexual assault case.

We drove to a local grammar school to interview a pre-teen about her allegations against her stepfather. I was stunned at how tiny and petite she was. The stature of the barely four-foot-tall frame of the twelve-year-old Hispanic female was typical of any child her age I guessed. Delicate and angelic were her facial features. She was a beautiful child, but cursed with being overdeveloped for her age, an objectifying physical trait.

Listening to her tiny voice describe how her younger sibling's father repeatedly entered her room each night filled me with sadness and anger.

I had known enough women to have heard similar stories and knew how common her plight was. It was understandable that the young minds of her barely school aged sibling would reject her claims. It was vile enough that the 12-year-old would have to live with her memories.

What was most difficult for me was imagining the guilt thrust upon the child because of her mother's refusal to believe her daughter's claims about her husband. Why would her child make up such a heinous crime?

I wanted to get up, go to her home, and shoot stepdaddy in the dick. It was difficult to watch her cry and shake as she relayed her story to us. She was forced into telling two strangers, adult men her story. It didn't matter that we were cops. If the dad were taken into custody, she would have to tell the story repeatedly to other necessary parties in the process.

I accepted that if she could be brave and share this story, I must be professional, take careful and accurate notes and be ready to do my job. The more shocking revelation of this situation was when I learned that because her perpetrator was a family member, a conviction would carry a less severe penalty. Less jail time and both were likely to return to the same home, the theory being, the victim is better off with family, versus a stranger. The law is a strange thing sometimes.

My trainer congratulated me afterwards for managing to keep my mouth shut during the process. All trainees were required to sit and observe, not interject. Afterwards, we stopped at the district station to pick up his partner, and my second trainer.

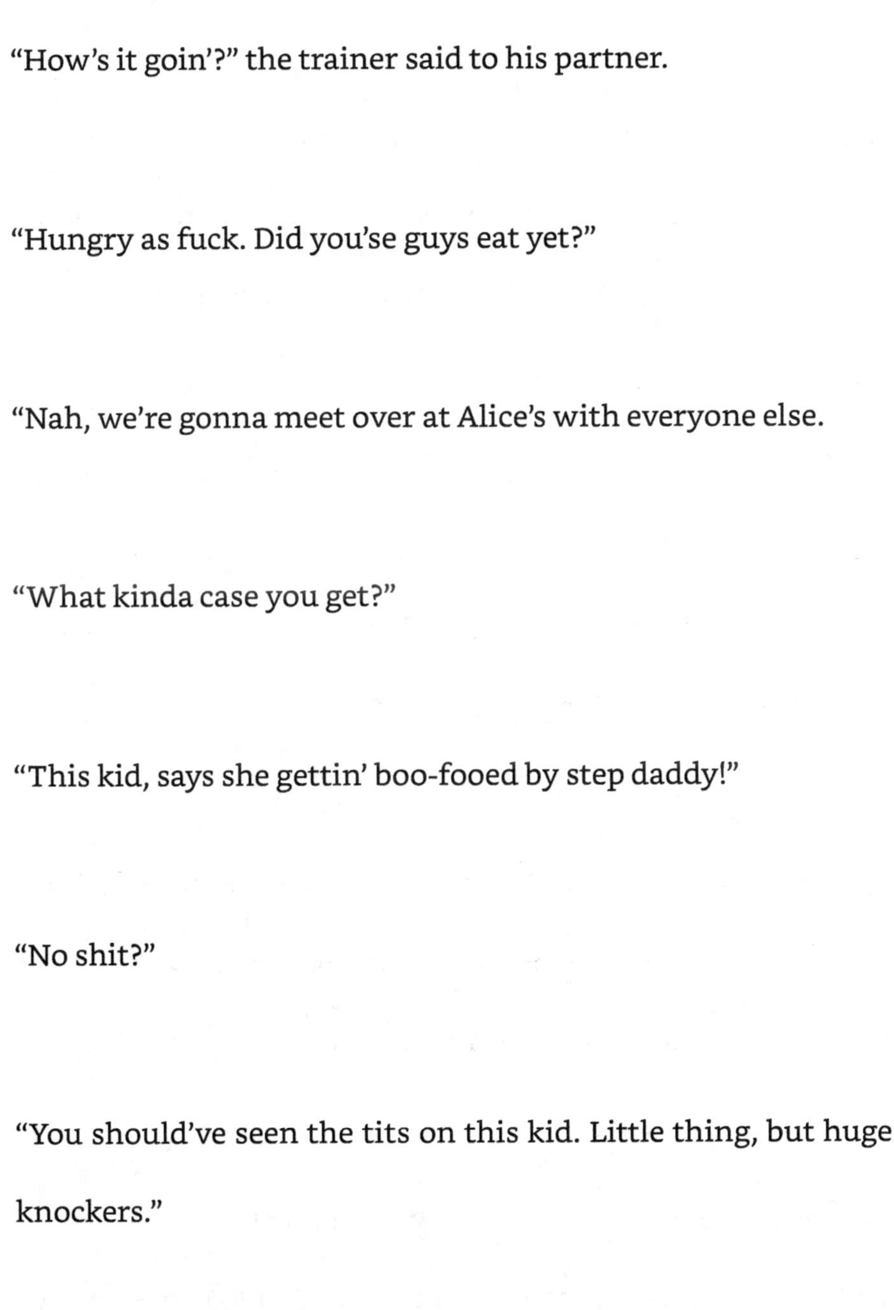

"How's it goin'?" the trainer said to his partner.

"Hungry as fuck. Did you'se guys eat yet?"

"Nah, we're gonna meet over at Alice's with everyone else.

"What kinda case you get?"

"This kid, says she gettin' boo-fooed by step daddy!"

"No shit?"

"You should've seen the tits on this kid. Little thing, but huge knockers."

I started to tune out their conversation. I wondered if they were carrying on like this to mask pain or were they really a couple of perverse bastards. As we rode towards the breakfast spot, I was snapped back to reality while we were stopped at a light.

I had taken the back seat of the unmarked squad car when my trainer picked up his partner. Across from us, a middle-aged Black man driving the car to the right of us looked at me with sadness in his eyes. The guys noticed.

"Hey, what's his face? Duke, show 'em your hands so he'll see that you're not in custody." The partner said as they both exploded with uncontrolled laughter. Fuckers.

We met at the breakfast spot with the other investigators and my co-workers. There were plenty of side conversations circulating the table. Soon we were up and rolling again, but the rest of the day breezed by. About an hour before quitting time, we returned to the station.

The trainers were chatting with friends, and I was doing my best to stay out of the way. I didn't know what to think about what I saw and heard that day, but my thought flashed back to the Homicide section of my academy training. We were urged to stay detached and objective to the situations we encountered. Maybe I was incapable of leaving the worst of this job in the streets.

The other team brought in a 16-year-old Black female. She was a runaway. I gathered from the conversation that she was dating a twenty-year-old who was a relative of one of her neighborhood friends. A uniformed beat came across her and now she was being held until her parents arrived.

Teenaged girls, I thought and shook my head. I remember times that I rode around with my mother as she searched the Westside of the city and our old stomping grounds in the projects for Sister. I'll never forget the look of desperation and fear in my mother's eyes and the tears that streamed down her face as each of my sister's friends and their parents told my mother sorry, "...but she hasn't been here," or "I haven't seen her at school today."

Teenaged girls: puberty calls and suddenly they think that they are wiser than their parents, slicker than their mother and unable to be swayed by anyone but their boyfriend. Darkness fell and Momma gave up the hunt and returned home to find my sister in her room pretending to do her homework. A cold glassy eyed stare came over my mother's face as she slowly walked into my sister's room and silently shut the door.

I rushed downstairs to listen through the floor and vents. I waited for the screaming and the well-deserved beating I would have given her if I were in my mother's shoes, but I didn't hear a thing. Maybe Momma talked with her quietly. Maybe they sat in the room in silence. Perhaps there wasn't a backlash because the sins of the daughter had hit too close to home.

I thought about my mother and sister. I reflected on the delicate child I listened to earlier in the shift and then I watched the runaway sitting quietly and waiting patiently for her folks.

I approached her. "You don't know me, and I probably should keep my opinion to myself, but no matter how bad you think life is right now, or whatever it is you are searching for, the safest place for you is home. No one will ever love you or worry about you the way that your family will. You're growing up but take your time and try to think about your choices." I said to her.

She never looked up. She just continued to look at the floor and rock her legs. Her parents walked in minutes after I finished my speech, but I soon found out that the teen wasn't my only

audience. I wasn't loud, but my trainers and a few of their

counterparts heard me loud and clear.

"So, are you gonna save her? Is that what you think we are

doing here?"

"No." I said as I felt my temper starting to flash.

"I just I wanted to say something.

"If you wanna do social work, this ain't the place!" He said as he

leaned into my personal space.

"I think that's the one thing I'm clear about." I said as I smiled

and leaned in closer to his face.

As I drove home from the Westside, I passed by the streets, and locations I had seen from the window of our car, or from buses my entire life. The dirty, drunk, and poverty-stricken people hangout, and wander aimlessly though life. Nothing but the passage of time has changed. It's a good thing the unit folded without Mayo. Otherwise, I would have been forced to quit.

My stint as a Juvenile Officer put me on the Chief's radar and opened an opportunity for me to apply to Internal Inspections. This was also short-lived. It was the brainchild of George Murray, our second Chief who was previously with the Illinois State Troopers. He wanted to rid our rank and file of the problem police officers and eliminate allegations of corruption. He was well intentioned in this endeavor. No one likes snitches. Even when it's obviously the right thing to do. Whistle blowers, regulators anyone who seeks to correct and hold another accountable is seen as a snitch. That is exactly what our fellow patrolmen saw us as.

"Snitches on deck!" Officers would shout out whenever we came into a station. Usually, the mood was lighthearted, and I accepted it as friendly ribbing, but it got old after a while.

We were asked to purchase our command stars. Our investigator badge resembled the ones worn by CPD's top brass. As soon as they saw it, it was like goodbye arrogance, hello ass kissing.

Most citizens of Chicago are unaware that only has authority to write traffic citations on the city streets and on Lake Shore Drive. CPD would write their own mother if they were to catch her going one mile over the speed limit, but the expressways belong to the state troopers.

Once when I was running late to a meeting with the Chief, I was bending the sound barrier and saw CPD riding parallel to me in the express lane. Since I was close to the office, I dropped down to about five miles per hour over the speed limit and continued to roll with the faster morning rush hour traffic.

I watched merge over into the local lane and get behind me. He followed closely for about a mile before he hit his lights and siren. "Dammit!" I thought. I was minutes away from making it into the meeting in the nick of time. I stopped and opened my car door to approach the officer.

"Get back in the vehicle! Get your ass back in the vehicle now!" He screamed over the mic.

"I'm sorry! I'm just running late." I said as I moved my jacket to allow him to see my star.

How his eyes bulged as they focused on the gold of my star from almost twenty feet away surprised me, but the officer was like instant pussy, add water and stir.

"Oh, I'm sorry sir! You go ahead! My mistake! Have a great day!

He shouted as he hopped back into his vehicle and sped away.

There was another incident that involved a patrolman who worked the lock up at CPD's 021st District. The officer refused to return my calls, so I stopped at the station to see if he could be located. I walked in and introduced myself to the desk personnel and asked if I could speak with the watch commander. I received a very unexpected greeting.

Instead of being escorted behind the desk by a patrolman, the lieutenant came out of his office to get me.

"Yes sir, welcome to my station. Would you like to step into my office?" He said as he held the door open for me.

He was more than polite and extremely professional with me because of the star I was wearing. He promised full co-operation from the officer I sought and arranged to have someone relieve him and to find us a room so that I could interview him.

It felt good to be treated well, yet the memories of other occasions where I had been treated so badly inside their station made the feelings of satisfaction bittersweet. However, doing my job on my own timetable and being treated with respect was far better than being on patrol.

I was pulled onto the team by a good friend and former boss of mine, Sergeant Whatley. It allowed us to work together again on serious matters and fuck off royally when there was down time. However, Whatley was never beyond answering calls for shots fired, or any other hot call. I was wearing my best suits to work. I didn't want to be wrestling and chasing fools the way we did when we were in uniform. When I was working with Whatley, it wasn't my call.

One hot Saturday night there was a call of shots fired at 141 N. Wolcott. The perpetrators were targeting the police. Whatley came up on the mic and let dispatch know that Inspections were in route.

Rolling northward up Wolcott towards Lake, we can see about eight of CPD's finest huddled on the northern corner of 1847 W. Lake St., the sister attached building to 141 N. Wolcott. With live gunfire coming from an apartment on a higher floor, Whatley calls dispatch.

"Put us out of the vehicle at 141 N. Wolcott!"

"Oh shit." I said as he parked us right in front of the building and got out of the car.

I quickly exited behind him and drew my weapon in sync with his. CPD waved at us to get out of the way as they huddled along the outer wall. We started to jog towards the darkened lobby to do what housing paid us for. We separated in the stairwell as CPD finally grew some balls and followed us into the building to search for our trigger-happy shooters. Shotgun blasts were heard as we reached the higher floors, but we found nothing.

Unknown to me at the time, most apartments were vacant in both buildings. Like rats, the thugs used sledgehammers to knock holes in the cinderblock walls. Those holes allowed them to enter one building and escape through the next.

As CPD and other CHAPD officers arrived on the scene to search the apartments, Whatley called us clear, and we exited the building. It was good to feel the rush again and even better to show CPD how to be the police.

In the seconds before exiting the vehicle to back up my partner I remembered that we get shot at every day and hiding in the shadows was not the way to break the gangbangers grip. You must take the fight to them and that's what Whatley wanted to do.

Later that evening we stopped by the ABLA station to check in on the watch commander. I heard laughter coming from the lock up area, so I peeked in to investigate.

"Oh shit! Snitches! Snitches!" the officer said.

"Chill." I responded.

"What do you have?" I asked.

"This old funky motherfucker over here, a homeless bastard that's about to get this Criminal Trespass to State Supported Land." He replied.

"What he needs is some soap with his dirty ass! Damn, how can you go for days without washing your ass?" his partner chimed in sarcastically.

"Be cool!" I said as I stepped closer to the derelict in cuffs.

I immediately recognized him, and I said his name.

"Otis?"

"You know this stanky mug?" The officer said as they laughed louder.

"The fuck's wrong with you all? This is a person. Maybe just a shell, but still a person. We played together as kids. I haven't seen him since I was a teen. Stop treating him like this and process your paperwork, before I put paper on you!" I said, as the room fell quiet.

I looked back at Otis once more before I walked out of the holding area and out of the station. What a sad twist of fate.

The caramel complexioned and hazel eyed basketball playing wizard who was the favorite of all the local girls had allowed himself to become a dingy cracked out non-entity. I stood there for a moment then it was time to go home. I had enough of walking down memory lane for one night.

As the department grew through new hires, each batch brought new stories and odd twists to our team dynamics. The first class pioneered us and was serious about our image and legacy. My class, the second class, wanted to prove ourselves worthy of the reputation and professionalism of the first class.

The third class were the rebels. They were younger and mirrored the general lack of prior policing skills of our class and regretfully were trained by individuals that wanted to be friends with their trainee, instead of making them prove themselves worthy of the star and our department.

In my opinion, the following classes and lateral transfers to our department were a mixed bag of personalities that were more prone to act upon their own personal agendas. We were slowly morphing into what was common to other lackluster police departments.

When I was still working on a uniformed beat, while waiting for a fresh battery for my radio, I overheard a conversation about a complainant from the ABLA Homes who reported that he had been the victim of a sexual assault.

The victim stated that a man approached him from behind and forced him at gunpoint to get into his car and drive to a secluded location. The victim was forced to get into the back seat, bend over and pull his pants down. The offender proceeded to lick the victim's anus, and then ran away. We all thought it was oddly hilarious.

"Don't you think he had that backwards?" an officer asked.

"You'd think since he had the gun, he'd make the victim lick his ass!" We laughed at the absurd tale, and I had forgotten about it.

I was having a boring shift and was the only car up for inspections. I didn't have anyone to interview, so I rolled around in my Impala and listened to the calls for service city-wide. There was little to no activity, so I decided to return to the office to update my paperwork.

"Excuse me, can I help you?" The security officer said as I entered the building.

"It's okay. I'm going up to Inspections." I said as I flashed my star.

"Well, you're going to have to sign my sheet."

"We don't sign in and out. I may be running in and out all night." I explained.

"I'm not trying to give you a hard time, but I was told to have everyone who enters the building to sign in." Security said as he stood his ground to my complaints.

"Fine." I said as I complied with his repeated requests.

I rode the elevator up and did not leave the building again until it was time for me to go home. I made sure that I was properly signed out before I left the building.

The next day, I found my commander waiting for me at my desk.

"Hey boss, shouldn't you be at home today?" I asked.

"Normally, but I was called in because we need to talk." He said.

"Okay, what do we need to discuss?" I questioned.

"Where were you last night? What were you wearing? What were you doing?" he asked as he twiddled his thumbs.

Oh shit, what did I do to make someone report me I wondered? I carefully and truthfully recanted the events of my previous shift. I told him about where I cruised, personal stops and about my conversations with security before the commander chimed in.

"Well signing in with security may have saved your ass." He

began.

"Last night, a woman walked into the Taylor Station with her sixteen-year-old son and reported that a police officer sexually assaulted him in a stairwell."

I was shocked and confused because I had not made the connection of why he was approaching me with the allegation.

"The teen said he was stopped in the stairwell by a male Black CHA Police officer who was wearing a brown leather jacket. He said the officer made him get down on his knees and perform oral sex on him at gunpoint." The only thing that immediately cleared you in my mind was the fact that the perpetrator had a mustache and goatee, which you do not have. Once I arrived at the office I saw the sign in sheet. You were here well before the incident and did not leave until after the report had been made." He said with a smile.

"Your ass was lucky." he said.

"But why would anyone suspect me?" I asked.

"The offender was alone, you were ninety-nine. The offender was CHAPD which was confirmed by the boy who said he was eye level to the star that was clipped onto the offender's belt. Besides, the guys working tactical last night were all saying you matched the description."

I couldn't believe that they thought this about me. Why would they say that I could be the perpetrator?

"Don't worry about it. I knew you couldn't have done it, but I had to ask."

I said I understood, but my pride was hurt. I had been a good cop and I thought I had an excellent record in the eyes of my peers, but I was wrong. A few weeks later, the Tactical Team members that pointed the finger at me were forced to ask themselves why none of them noticed the pedophile in their midst.

The real culprit was a fellow team member of their team, who I will call "Fudgins." Fudgins assaulted a teen drug dealer twice. The first time occurred inside a vacant apartment, and the second happened inside his personal vehicle. The youth disregarded Fudgins warnings against snitching. He went to CPD, and they issued the warrant for Fudgins arrest.

Later, the Tactical Team members joked about how little kids would point at Fudgins and call him the "Raper Man." They ignored the warning signs and pointed the finger in the wrong direction, but I still didn't feel vindicated.

THE RETURN

The authority did not renew Chief Murray's contract. A new leader was plucked from the ranks to take the reins of the department temporarily before the new Chief and chairman of HUD came aboard. Regardless, I was out of Inspections like yesterday's trash. Most of us were. It is the nature of office politics to play favorites over quality or substance. I really didn't mind returning to the street. Most of the perks were an illusion, and it was obvious that the experience I gained would never help me toward advancement in our department, or any other.

No one on the beat welcomed the "snitches" back into the ranks, so we all landed in various stations and special details. I was sent to the Evidence and Recovered Property Section, or ERPS. I worked there for about five months before I was returned to regular patrol. However, things were changing rapidly under the new chairman and Chief.

In the beginning, we were created as a supplement to CPD. We were there to perform above baseline services in our area of patrol. Because of the lack of cooperation, we received and the mounting animosity over the city's lack of support regarding how we accomplished our daily goals, the CHAPD branched out into other CPD Districts and started to develop specialized units.

At the same time, Vince Lane partnered with the LAC to target problem areas and pushed through projects that improved the visual setting of housing by restoring its amenities. During Lane's departure, the mayor was still working behind the scenes to regain control of public housing and the government funds funneled into our department to run it.

The discourse between the new Chief, Leroy O'Shield, and the media about the future of the CHAPD became muddled and unsure. He was quoted by local television media and in newsprint saying, "We are in the housing business," in response to a question about proposed layoffs within our ranks. My co-workers and I were sure that we would be needed as long as the high-rises existed. No one wanted to believe that the end could come so quickly.

HUD started a massive project to restore dilapidated buildings across the city, but especially in the Robert Taylor Homes. I do not know how much Public Housing spent during that period, but they fixed walls and repaired the vacant apartments. They repainted every unit, expanded the percentage of apartment doors to allow handicapped access to units, and even replaced the kitchen and bedroom lighting with ceiling fans. The project had to cost millions of dollars. The finished structures that sat as an example of what could be done to buildings city-wide were the first to implode.

It was the beginning of the end, and the writing on the walls crumbled and drifted away within the dusty clouds.

P.O.P.

I don't like to pick at people, but I do prefer to get the last laugh. After the arrest of an offender, who stood about two to three inches taller and approximately 30 to 40 pounds heavier than I was, he decided to give me some lip after the arrest. However, there is no law against insulting a cop.

As a law enforcement officer, your peace cannot be breached, or so the rules of conduct dictate. So, trash-talking civilians are free from harassment, detainment, or being taken into custody, unless they were disturbingly loud and drew a crowd, or spoke in a threatening manner to an officer, which would cause a reasonable person to believe that they were in danger of receiving a battery. Otherwise, it's hands off and the individual is protected by free speech. In the merry world of make believe this scenario may be possible, but in my experience and in the minds of other officers, loose lips may earn you anything from public embarrassment, or a well-whupped ass followed by a trip to the lock up.

My big thug decided to call me names and to scream loudly in my face while I wrote out his paperwork in our lock up area. Most of our workspaces served a dual purpose. Our lock up area was also part waiting room and employee cafeteria. As I continued to fill out the arrest report, the prisoner continued to taunt me. Suddenly, I stopped writing, pushed my reports to the side as I stared into his eyes.

"What? You gon' do somethin' nigga? You bad? Are you supposed to mad and gon do somethin'? Huh nigga? What?" he said to me.

I continued to stare at him blankly, then smiled when an idea came to mind.

"Oh, is somethin' supposed to be funny muthafucka? Yo pussy ass ain't gon do nuthin!" he said as he continued to berate me.

I ripped a strip of paper from a discarded report lying nearby and then slowly tore it into smaller pieces. As I started to roll the smaller pieces into little balls, the taunts and berating stopped and then turned into nervous inquiry.

"What's this shit?" he asked as I lined the little balls of paper up in front of me, yet directly across from him. Then there was complete silence. It was quiet enough to hear a church mouse pissin' on cotton.

As his eyes were transfixed on the row of little balls on the table, I flicked one at him by using my thumb and middle finger. Bulls-eye! The first shot hit him on his cheek, below his left eye. Bulls-eye again and again as I started to rapidly fire them at him, holding back my laughter as I repeatedly hit him about the face and neck with my miniature projectiles!

Frustrated, the prisoner let out a scream, "Aaaaaahhhh, goddammit!!! Stop it! Stop hittin' me wit that shit! Aaaaaahhhhh, I want the watch commander! Help! Help me somebody!" he said as I continued to pelt him with total accuracy as he pulled at his cuffed hands, weaved his head from side to side as he kicked his feet at me from under the table.

Soon the watch commander came out of his office to see what all of the yelling about, while I tried to act casual.

"What seems to be the problem?" the Sergeant asked.

"Nothing." I said calmly as my prisoner continued to buck around like a four-year-old throwing a temper tantrum.

"He keeps on hittin' me! Muthafucka I'll beat yo ass if I didn't have on these cuffs! Aaaahhhh!" he screamed again.

"I didn't touch him." I replied, as I casually leaned away from him while I sat on the opposite side of the table.

"Yes you did! Muthafucka yes you did! You kept popping me with that paper!" he continued, growing angrier and more frustrated by the second.

"I need to see you in my office." the sergeant said as I tried to explain that I couldn't leave him cuffed without someone to watch.

"Dukes, get in my office!" He commanded and I obeyed.

"What in the hell is wrong with you?" he asked me behind the closed doors.

"What?" I replied as I played the nut roll.

He let out a sigh and asked if my paperwork was ready for signatures, to which I replied yes. "Bring them to me so you can get his ass outta my station. I swear, dealing with you all is like babysitting a bunch of kids." He said.

As I walked out of the office with a big smile, my thug was

finally quiet. He slowly shook his head from side to side as the tears welled up in his eyes. A part of me wanted to continue to egg him on, but I could tell that he was at his breaking point. I wanted him to stop talking and taunting me and he was complying. I got the last laugh, and he learned not to Piss Off the Police.

RESIDENTS IN THE AFTERMATH

Once, while I was working "Hire back," an overtime program instituted to encourage officers to stay on for later shifts or to sign up to work on their days off, I had the opportunity to watch the residents and how they spent their days.

I grew up in an era where the project moms were older, more attentive to their children, and were on a quest to find work and a way out of poverty. The new residents, who were the children and grandchildren of my generation, were young, wild, and foul. Every day was playtime. From sunup to sundown, I watched the current generation awaken and roam the building around 10 a.m., come down to the lobby, or playground to visit with friends while their non-school-aged children played.

During the summer months, they chased one another up and down the stairs and utilized balloons or buckets to have water fights. Around noon, most would disappear into their apartments to eat or send someone on a run to a local fast-food spot for something greasy but delicious.

Around 2 p.m., they would load up their cars and head toward the lakefront or cruise around their neighborhood, never venturing too far for fear of rival gang members. At sunset, or later, they returned to the parking lot to laugh, fight, or to play some more. Things would slow down around 2 a.m. Most would return to their apartments to be alone with their lovers, friends, or to sleep. Around 10 a.m., the cycle would begin again.

I asked myself, "Why would anyone living this way crave more?" The life of a drug dealer is violent, but not everyone sold drugs, used drugs, or were gang members. Strip away the dirty apartments, the violent atmosphere, and the stigma of receiving public aid, and what do you have? A paid and extended vacation!

Only the elite, the truly wealthy get to decide when and if they want to work. They can decide for themselves. The youth of public housing led an existence that watched their parents and family members receive food and shelter for free. Lacking education and disregarding housing rules did not stop the free ride. Even imprisonment failed to be a deterrent to following the status quo of the environment they lived in. Why would anybody want to struggle for necessities and deal with the hustle and bustle of the workforce, terrible bosses, long

commutes, or higher education when they could relax and live

stress-free?

LAST DAYS

ince Lane was gone, and the City of Chicago was given control of our department. When the first group of patrolmen and supervisors were laid off, the writing on the wall became clear. The city planned to move the residents out, destroy the buildings and dismantle the department, but not necessarily in that order. Nothing was going to stop housing's plan to tear down public housing and do away with the CHAPD. We and the projects were being knocked down one by one. I cannot say which was more painful to watch, the elimination of my tangible personal history, or my future in law enforcement. What was even scarier was the way the residents were being uprooted and cast aside.

My latest partner, Tanya and I were one of the teams that were assigned the duty of informing residents that they would be evicted if they did not pay their past due balance on their rent. I was surprised to learn that most people paid less than thirty dollars a month for rent. However, most owed thousands of dollars because housing allowed them to go for years without taking action to collect or evict. One woman had over five thousand dollars' worth of past due payments. There was no way a truly poor person could ever raise that much money to pay that balance. In retrospect, it was probably best for all of those who could not pay, or refused to try because they were eventually evicted anyway.

The next wave of housing's assault on evicting their poor came in the form of closing buildings that had been left in disrepair for decades, under the guise of "health and comfort." The media were allowed to enter apartments and televise the sweaty cobweb-filled walls of super-heated apartments and to tape footage of huge holes in drywall that extended into neighboring apartments and allowed the free rein of the project's super rats and roaches to roam and prey on sleeping victims.

Like our department, public housing rarely received any positive press. When housing was trying to rid itself of the gangs, violence and graffiti, the coverage was negative, or attributed to CPD. Suddenly, it was okay for the Authority and the local media to show the conditions the residents were faced with daily. Usually, a disgruntled resident invited local news reporters into their apartments to show how the authority was falling short with repairs. The tenants probably thought that letting their cluttered and roach-filled homes be televised would bring about change and upgrades to their living conditions. All it did was further convince the general public that the buildings were a blight upon the city that had to be destroyed.

I never liked it when I read the newspaper and saw how they portrayed public housing as "warehouses for the poor" or used prison terms like "lockdown" to describe situations where we were trying to monitor who was visiting housing's property. Most multi-unit apartment complexes have buzzers installed to restrict the flow of non-residents. High-rise apartments on the Gold Coast and downtown have doormen that challenge visitors to their property. They said that poor people cannot be allowed to live in close quarters and be expected to behave civilly. I challenge any apartment dweller or homeowner to make the claim that they have not had to deal with a neighbor or others in the community that were inconsiderate and made living amongst them difficult. People are just assholes to each other sometimes. Money and influence do not change that fact.

As a remedy to allowing the residents to continue to live in the "dangerous" environments they endured for a decade, housing rented rooms in local hotels. This did not go well.

Devoid of any "home training" for decades, the residents were accused of getting high in their hallways, using the stairwells as a toilet, throwing parties in the rooms, and fighting over which gang would control the hotel to which they were assigned.

I found it hard to condemn their behavior because they had been allowed to live that way for so long and it was tolerated. Why should anyone be surprised that the residents wouldn't change their regular behavior, because they were in new surroundings?

Soon, most of the hotels in the Chicagoland area refused to take the residents in or accept housing's money. Housing was able to sucker a few suburban motel owners to accept the residents, but that was also short-lived. After the media ran stories about the residents' antics, most refused to deal with them. However, there were plenty of tricks to come.

The final ploy involved issuing vouchers to the residents and enticing suburban townships to take them in. The authority was supposed to be replacing the high-rise buildings with low-rise townhouses, similar to the plans used in the beginning of housing's history. However, there would not be a matching number of units, which meant a percentage of the residents would still be displaced.

While on assignment at one of CHA's branch offices, I listened in on a session of meetings they had with the residents to inform them of how the vouchers would work and about the pending demise of all the high-rise developments. Most of the residents that attended were of limited education. Many did not know how to write a check, manage money through a checking or savings account and other affairs most adults are accustomed to doing.

There was a glazed empty stare on the faces of the motley crowd of men and women present. Most did not seem to understand what they were being told, or what they could do about it. The dissatisfaction and fear of being on their own and the responsibility for their own care was evident.

I knew that it was their fault that they were in this situation. They made the wrong choices in life and had allowed a greater entity control of their welfare. Now that the powers that be no longer wanted them as a voting block or as a headache, the residents were learning the folly of such decisions. They were being cast aside because they were no longer of any use.

Housing also allowed them to stay on their property because occupied units for profits sake outweighed having responsible tenants. If money could be generated under the guise of assisting the poor, the most wretched of the residents would be welcome to call public housing home. As soon as the city and public housing knew that they could tear down the buildings, sell the land to developers willing to pay huge sums of money to build beautiful dwellings to bring the elite back into the inner city from local suburbs, it was over. Plain and simple, money talks, poor people kick rocks.

Eventually, housing moved the residents out by giving them vouchers and a pat on the head. A select few were relocated to other buildings as most were boarded up and immediately knocked down. Eventually, they were all pushed off housing's property.

As the buildings fell and the residents disappeared, we were also being picked apart. Chief O'Shield seemed devoid of sympathy when the authority wanted to diminish the size and manpower of the CHAPD. However, he seemed distraught when he and his crew were ousted by Mayor Daley's latest tool, CPD's Transition Team. Harvey Radney came aboard as the last Chief of CHAPD. He brought with him a team of officers to investigate our staff, assess our assets.

One of the first things the city wrested control of was our Evidence and Recovered Property.

All the weapons that we had confiscated and held pending cases were destroyed. The drugs we confiscated were transferred to CPD's Evidence and Recovered Property

Section, (ERPS), and the drug money was deposited into an account that the city would control.

Our department leaders were made subordinate to the ranking officers from CPD, and this continued until our officers were patrolling ninety-nine in a one-man car or working a fixed post as security. CHA Security and most contract security firms were quickly eliminated. Because of the inherent dangers of working in public housing, we never worked ninety-nine. We no longer had a voice or a say, just orders that we could follow or quit. CPD had finally reduced us to a form that could no longer challenge or embarrass them.

I accepted the changes. Initially, I worried when I entered buildings without backup from a partner, or when I knew the watch had limited resources, but luckily, I had built a reputation that kept me safe. However, a boss and good friend could not do the same.

He was a friend of a friend in many ways. We crossed paths on the job. Once, while we were working "Hire back," he was notified that he had made the rank of sergeant. He was so proud, and I was happy for him. As a young single guy, I idolized his lifestyle. He was always dressed to the 9's, he drove a nice car and had an apartment in a high rise overlooking the lake. But, when he learned that he would not only be stripped of his rank, but he would also be fired, He made a grave decision. After a long night of drinking, he retired to his car in the parking lot of his favorite night spot and shot himself in the head. I later learned that he had heard that he was named in an investigation that was to net several officers on extortion and other crimes. In any case, it saddened me that suicide was the only escape he saw as an option to CPD's siege and final strike at members of our department.

The lieutenants and sergeants, mostly ex-CPD retirees who were already fully vested in pensions from both departments, per their contracts, bumped down in rank. Their actions pushed the latest batch of sergeants back into the rank of patrolman. They were the first to be laid off. Not reading the small print of a contract gets you every time.

Everything was changing around me. When I became a police officer, I was young, single, and believed wholeheartedly that I had found the occupation that I would pursue until retirement. But as our department was wrested away from us, we, like the buildings we patrolled, we were being dismantled piece by piece. In the end, I found myself in middle-age, a new father facing the possibilities of divorce, and totally disillusioned about my ability and desire to continue a career in law enforcement. I was changing. I wasn't as brave and accepting of the possibilities of death due to the job. I wanted to go home to my child. I always believed that once your mind was no longer on the people and the task, it's time to go. I was less patient with people and my ability to provide those short-term solutions to lifelong problems. Sadly, I was also becoming bitter and petty. I was just short of ten years on the job, and I was done.

Very few of the officers I spoke with on a regular basis were interested in employment with suburban departments. Many of the white officers had grown accustomed to the action and adrenaline they found in the gutters of Chicago's most dangerous environments. They couldn't go back to the quieter days on a suburban beat.

Meanwhile, the Black officers recognized that the suburban townships welcoming them with open arms would do so because of their need for officers specialized in quelling the level of violence their small-town forces had yet to master. However, we all knew that no other department in the state would come close to paying us the salaries we had grown accustomed to, except CPD.

"Goin' wit da 'titty' was never a consideration for me in the end. Early in my career, I sought an escape from the apathy of our leadership and considered switching departments. After years of patrol and dealing with all levels of the CPD hierarchy, I couldn't accept the octagon patch and checkerboard hat band in good conscience. Like some of my fellow officers, I contemplated leaving the state to further my career.

Officer Soros married one of our dispatchers and moved away out east with her to continue policing. The year he served on his new department must have been very impressive. Soros was urged to recruit officers from our department who were willing to relocate. I thought about the possibilities, but I did not want to move across the country and leave my son behind.

I was lost without the dreams I had built around my family, but unless I wanted to return to being a file clerk for the VA, I had to determine the best use of my marketable skills. Rumors of our pending demise increased as the months dragged on, and more developments were ground into powder.

Simultaneously, my personal life was unraveling at a similar rate. I drove up to Hatfield, Wisconsin, on every three-day weekend I had to spend time with my little man. Each time I saw him, he was a little bigger and more skillful. In my absence, he learned to walk.

I reminisced about the pockets of peaceful times we had before our latest breakup. My wife and I would take turns holding our child in a standing position as we urged our little one to walk between us. We cheered and laughed at the thumping sound of the diapered bottom with each fall. Those weekends seemed so short compared to the four-plus hours it took to complete the one-way drive.

Back in Chicago, I no longer needed to rush home, because the only things waiting for me were darkness and quiet. Sometimes, I wouldn't bother to turn on a lamp, or hit a light switch. I would sit on the couch and doze, or lie in bed with my entire uniform on.

I recalled how the light rumble of my wife's throat, and the lamb-like bay of my baby's snore would sound in sync with one another. In my solitude, the only sounds that occupied the house were the beatings of my heart, and the creaking and settling of my 70-year-old home.

THE CHOICE

all was settling in on the city, and my one-man patrol of Beat 2842 had been uneventful so far.

"Beat 2842."

"Go for 42."

"Return to the Taylor Station and see the watch commander, 10-4?"

"In route to Taylor squad."

Now what had I done? I rushed back to the station and nervously approached the watch commander's office, replaying the day's events in my mind for clues as to why I was summoned.

"Close the door," Sgt. Drink said.

"What's up, Sarge?" I asked, trying to hide my nervousness.

"Dukes, you need to call your wife. I received a call that your son has been hospitalized."

My mouth went dry, and my stomach sank as my mind raced through wild conclusions about what could have happened to my baby boy.

"Do you know what happened? What did she say?"

"Dukes, go and call your wife! Let me know if you will need time off, and I will take your car down."

"Yeah, you can do that now, because I'm about to get on the road right now!"

I did not go home. I just jumped on Interstate 90/94 west and drove as fast as I could until I arrived at Black River Falls Hospital, 270 miles away. My wife and my in-laws were already at bedside. My baby was lying there, under the plastic cover that encased the bed, holding onto the railings. He had pneumonia, but the doctors expected full recovery. His asthma was not helping his current condition, but he was as comfortable as could be expected. My mom lost a baby to pneumonia. My brother Nathan was born two years before me. He was 11 months old when it took him. His loss had a profound effect on her. Now, I'm afraid and concerned for my baby.

I sat there, staring at my baby lay under the transparent tarp. I thought about how this could have been worse. It could have resulted in death. Weeks earlier, my wife told me that she wanted us to reconcile. She suggested that I move to Wisconsin and look for work there in Black River.

Long before we met, I vowed never to leave Chicago. Making my home in another state was out of the question. Then again, things were changing. If my family was as important to me as I thought it was, then this was the only way to reunite it. I picked up a few applications around town and applied with local law enforcement agencies before I left to return home to

Chicago.

A week after I applied for jobs in Wisconsin, I returned to Black River Falls for an interview with the Compliance Department of the Ho Chunk Nation for the position of Drug Enforcement Agent. The following week, I received an offer of employment, and I accepted it. Eager to share my good news with my partner, Sara, I dragged her outside of the station.

"I'm up outta this mutha-fucka, Sara!" I said.

"What are you talking about? They gonna finally fire your ass before the end of CHA?" She cracked back.

"Funny. NOT! No, I got a job offer in Wisconsin, and I accepted it. I'll take a little bit of a pay cut, but the cost of living is better there. I'm about to go downtown and give them notice that in two weeks I'm out!" I informed her.

"Oh, hell no! You will not be leaving me here. You need to take me on a run." She exclaimed.

"Where you gotta go? I have to do this first." I replied.

"Oh, it's all good. I just need to get down to the Board of Education." She said.

Sara and I laughed all the way as we drove downtown from the projects, towards CHA's headquarters. Once inside, I was informed by a member of CHA's Human Resources that I did not want to quit.

He said, with a slight whisper, "You didn't hear this from me, but you all are going to get a severance package. If you quit now, you won't be getting anything. If you have any vacation time, take it, and stand by."

I thanked him for the info, and put my formal exit on hold. Once we got back to our car, I passed on the information to Sara. She was surprised, to say the least.

"Oh, fuck this! Take me over to the board right now!" Sara exclaimed.

I sat in the car, monitoring the radio for 15 minutes as I waited for her to return. Wearing her usual grimace, she came back to the car, and reached into the inside of her jacket to pull out a surprise.

"Taa-daa! This is what the fuck I'm talkin' about, Dukie!" she said with a chuckle.

She had a picture ID. Sara had just become an employee of the Board of Education.

"As much as I hate dealing with these little bad-assed kids, and their ghetto-assed mamas, I need to keep a job. I hope their mamas discipline them before I have to."

"Alright! Don't get fired, and go to jail!"

"I know that's right!" Sara said as we gave each other a high five.

We escaped CHA, and had beaten CPD at its own game. A slight chill of relief ran down the curve of my spine as I thought about how close we came to being unemployed. The pending fate of our comrades had not yet dawned on me. Less than a week after securing our exodus, the mayor authorized Chicago's Chief of Police to pull manpower from various districts to enter our five police stations to take control.

A friend told me that we, the CHAPD were CPD for about an hour, until our Housing Chairman tried, and failed to use the takeover of our police personnel as a bargaining chip to secure a position for himself with the city. East Coast boy didn't know how Chicago politics worked. We were given a red wedding, and his head was lopped off first!

The city was getting the money back that was used to fund our department. It was also poised to gain a well-trained army to disburse across the city to bolster its forces, but once again, politics and bullshit was knocking us down. We made more money than the average CPD officer, regardless of rank, and we did not have to live in the city. These were two things that the city did not want to fight the unions on. It was easier, so they thought, to send us on our way.

COPS #000 SPECIAL EDITION
"THE ROLE YOU PLAYED STAYS ON MY MIND."
I'M SCARED! I GOTTA PEE!!
I GOTTA PEE!
BRAH!
BETTA GIT YO ASS OUT DAIR AND DID YO DAM JOB!!
SOMEWHERE IN PUBLIC HOUSING...
C.H.A. I WAS THINKING HOW GOOD IT WAS WHEN YOU WERE HERE.
WE SERVE NO COLLECT
CHICAGO POLICE
AND IT AIN'T THE WINE THAT I'VE BEEN DRINKING, FOR ONCE I FEEL MY HEAD IS CLEAR.
RIPPLE
OOOHH
YEAH!
SINCE EARLY THIS MORNING WHEN I OPENED UP MY EYES...
FUC DA POLICE
GDS
THAT OLD LONESOME FEELING TOOK ME BY SURPRISE...
I GUESS YOU MEAN MORE TO ME THAN I REALIZED!
I'M NOT GOO TO POPO!
HACK!
I AIN'T GOIN TO JAIL!
THE ROLE YOU PLAYED STAYS ON MY MIND, THE LOVE WE LOST STAYS ON MY MIND.
AND C.H.A. I WAS TIRED, OF BUILDING CHECKS AND OTHER THINGS.
OOH TAKE YO TIME
OUR SIGHTS OF YOU DON'T HAVE ANY MEANING...
...AND MEMORIES ARE EVERYWHERE!
ROBO
OH YO MAMA
OOOH YEAH!
NOW I'M NOT COMPLAINING NAH
CURSE, THAT'S HOW IT GOES!
KAPOW!
THERE'S ALWAYS SOME HEARTACHE IN THIS WORLD I SUPPOSE!
OOH EEH HEE HOOO
NOW YOU CAN IMAGINE WHAT NOBODY KNOWS! NOBODY KNOWS ROBO!
YOUR ROLE STAYS ON OUR MINDS!
OH YES IT IS!
EEEEEEH HEEHEE EEH EE
MUCH LUV DOG GOOD-BYE.
CHICAGO HOUSING AUTHORITY DEPARTMENT OF POLICE
C.H.A FLYER

AS TOLD BY AN OFFICER AT ALTGELD GARDENS:

 Chicago Police Lieutenant, accompanied by an army of CPD patrolmen, filed into the Altgeld Gardens station.

"Sergeant, are you the watch commander?"

"Yes, what's all of this?"

"Call all your units into the station, and tell them to clean out their lockers! You're fuckin' done!" the Lieutenant said with a smile.

This scenario played out all over the city, and at every CHA Police Station. Simultaneously, CHA Administration personnel were calling officers at home to give us instructions about how the layoff would proceed.

I was off work, and missed the telecast of the media circus that showed the pained expressions, and tears of my co-workers. After 10 years of service in an environment that no one believed could be policed, the least we deserved was to be treated as professionals.

CHAPTER 8 – IN THE END

A week before I started working for the Ho Chunk Nation, in Black River Falls Wisconsin, as their Drug Enforcement Agent, I returned to Chicago for a meeting, and media coverage event hosted by the City Council. In that meeting, they discussed how the department would be dismantled, and the fate of its remaining officers and staff. Officers were allowed to speak about their experiences, the residents, and their expectations, after all the years they served protecting the community. The media broadcast snippets and sound bites that made our departure appear to be less of an injustice.

We were well paid, but like most Americans, only a few pay checks away from losing everything. Most people live above and beyond their means. We were no different. Officers were losing their homes, and everything they worked for with the stroke of a pen. There was one last photo opportunity the housing authority used our officers for. They lied to us! They said that there would be multiple departments waiting to hire our officers on as lateral transfers. The event failed to bring in more than a couple of suburban departments that were only "accepting applications."

Tested by time, the men and women of the defunct Chicago Housing Authority Police Department proved that they were truly the "real police." Ninety percent of them found employment with other law enforcement agencies, with seventy-five percent of our manpower taking on the checkerboard and octagon of CPD.

The remaining officers returned to public life as teachers, bus drivers, postal workers, or small business owners. Fewer still, were those who answered the call to assist as police in war-ravaged Bosnia, or in military service in the Middle East. Perhaps the allure of action, excitement, and danger found on the violent beats of the projects was too tempting of a mistress to let go of.

As for CPD, I was told by a friend that lateraled to the city after the majority of project buildings were demolished, that Chicago Police Officers were still whining on the radio whenever dispatch gave them a call for service in, and around public housing. Shulla told me she heard the dispatcher say, "Unit, CHAPD is gone. This is your job!" Tickled me to the bone! Scary asses!

I found solitude, for a short time anyway, in the rolling hills, and greenery of small-town Wisconsin. Being the odd man out was not difficult, as I had experienced it on different levels during my military service. Regardless of the negative racial bias from my new neighbors, people tended to be cordial at best, or silent at the very least. No one bothered me, and I didn't bother them.

I stood in contrast to the norms of Hatfield's relaxed, rural, slow-paced setting. Grocery shopping was eight miles away, dry cleaning had to be sent to a town fifty miles away, and fast food was limited to a choice between McDonald's or Burger King. Chicago spoiled me. No more Harold's Tasty Fried Chicken, Lem's Barbeque, Chi Tung's Chinese food, Schrimp from Laurence's, or Ricobene's chicken fried steak. Maybe a local fish fry or two from the local VFW was the best I could do in Black River, if I was lucky. However, home and family were my primary concerns now. I focused on starting anew with my wife, and on becoming the best father I could be for my child. Still, I pondered what the future would bring.